Cloth Doll
FACES

Acknowledgements & thanks

Many thanks to June Evans and Alan Lambert for their help in reading through my work, for all their encouragement and for their very special friendship.

Thanks to Vivienne Rudd, friend and guinea pig, and another brain in my hour of need.

Thanks to Marie Flanagan, fellow textile artist and fabric feeler.

Also many thanks to Pat and the late Ken Lumsdale, who through the years have given me much support and encouragement, which I have greatly valued and appreciated.

A special thank you to Pauline Millar, who started me on the road to doll making and who continues to share her expertise and friendship.

Finally, thanks to all my students whose enthusiasm and dedication inspire me to keep on designing and making new dolls year after year.

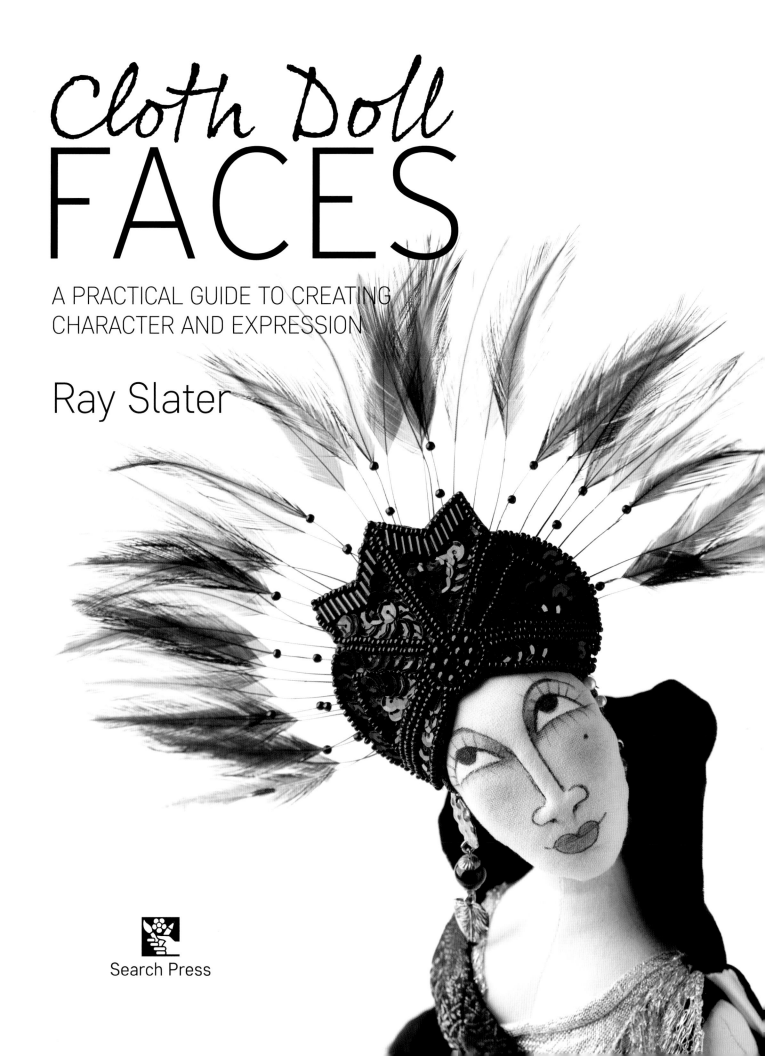

Cloth Doll
FACES

A PRACTICAL GUIDE TO CREATING CHARACTER AND EXPRESSION

Ray Slater

Search Press

First published in 2021

Search Press Limited
Wellwood, North Farm Road,
Tunbridge Wells, Kent TN2 3DR

Text, pattern templates, drawings and diagrams copyright
© Ray Slater 2021

Photographs by Paul Bricknell (pages 1, 3, 4, 5, 6–7, 8, 9, 10,
11, 13, 15, 26, 27, 31, 32, 33, 35b, 36b, 37, 38, 39, 40, 41, 49br,
57, 58, 60, 61, 62b, 63, 64b, 65, 66b, 67, 68, 69, 70, 71, 72, 73,
74, 75, 76b, 77, 78tr + l, 79, 80b, 81, 82, 83, 84, 85, 86, 87, 89,
90, 91, 92t, 93, 94, 95, 96tr, 97, 98tr + bl, 99, 100tr + bl, 101,
103–104, 104bl, 105, 106, 107, 108, 109, 110, 111, 112, 113, 114, 115,
116, 117) and Gavin Sawyer at Roddy Paine's Studios (pages
2, 16–17, 21, 23, 35t, 36t, 42, 43, 44, 45, 46, 47, 48, 49, 50, 51, 52,
53bg, 54, 55, 59, 62tr, 64t, 66tr, 76tl, 78br, 80tr, 88, 92br, 96b,
98br, 100br).

Photographs and design copyright © Search Press Ltd. 2021

Photographs on pages 18, 19 and 20 were taken by and are
the copyright of the author.

ISBN: 978-1-78221-307-9
ebook ISBN: 978-1-78126-344-0

SUPPLIERS
If you have difficulty in obtaining any of the materials and
equipment mentioned in this book, then please visit the
Search Press website for details of suppliers:
www.searchpress.com

You are invited to visit the author's website:
www.rayslaterclothdolls.co.uk

PUBLISHER'S NOTE
All the step-by-step photographs in this book feature the
author demonstrating how to make the faces and bodies of
the dolls. No models have been used.

The projects in this book have been made using metric
measurements, and the imperial equivalents provided
have been calculated following standard conversion
practices. The imperial measurements are often
rounded to the nearest $\frac{1}{16}$in for ease of use except in
rare circumstances; however, if you need more exact
measurements, there are a number of excellent online
converters that you can use. Always use either metric or
imperial measurements, not a combination of both.

SAFETY NOTICE
These dolls are not designed as play dolls and, because
of the small parts involved, are not suitable for children
under five years old.

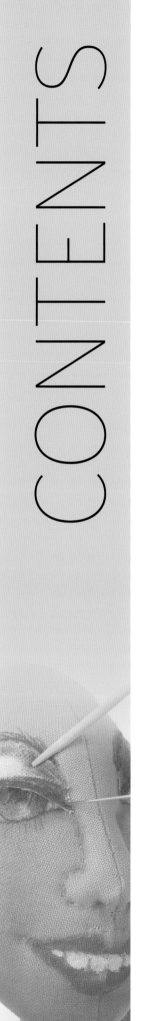

CONTENTS

INTRODUCTION

*'The face is one of the most important parts of
a doll, and it is its design that will determine
the figure's character.'*

For me, one of the most exciting and rewarding aspects of doll making is finding ideas for new faces and translating them into original designs. This book, therefore, focuses in part on where to look for inspiration, as well as how to adapt what you find to your own cloth creations.

I will explore several different techniques for creating a face or character. There is no need for complex drawing skills; by using the simplest line drawings you can develop a range of expressions and personalities. A line drawing is a very versatile and effective technique, and many different characters can be created using this simple method.

Drawing a realistic face requires a very different technique. It relies on the observation of human characteristics and the application of colour to develop light and dark tones which give depth and dimension to the face. Many people find the idea of drawing a face daunting – their reactions range from worried to terrified! I hope that the techniques and processes I demonstrate in this book will help to dispel those fears, enable you to become more relaxed and enjoy the process of designing and creating your own original doll face.

The decorative techniques used to turn your artwork into three-dimensional, fully formed faces are probably the most versatile and exciting. This is partly because there is an almost limitless supply of source material for inspiration, and partly because you can use a variety of media to create decorative effects. Applying dimensional features to a face results in the creation of a group of fun, characterful dolls and opens up possibilities for many future projects.

As you read through these pages, remember that every new skill takes practice. Be patient and enjoy the journey.

Ray x

Face & doll-making notions

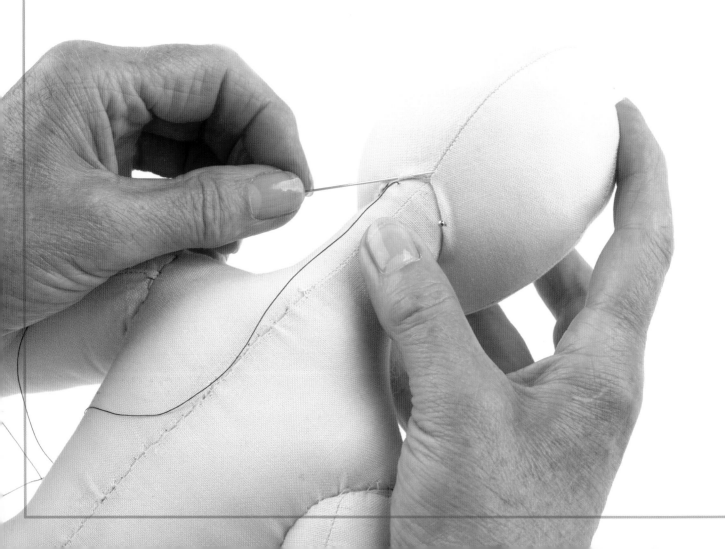

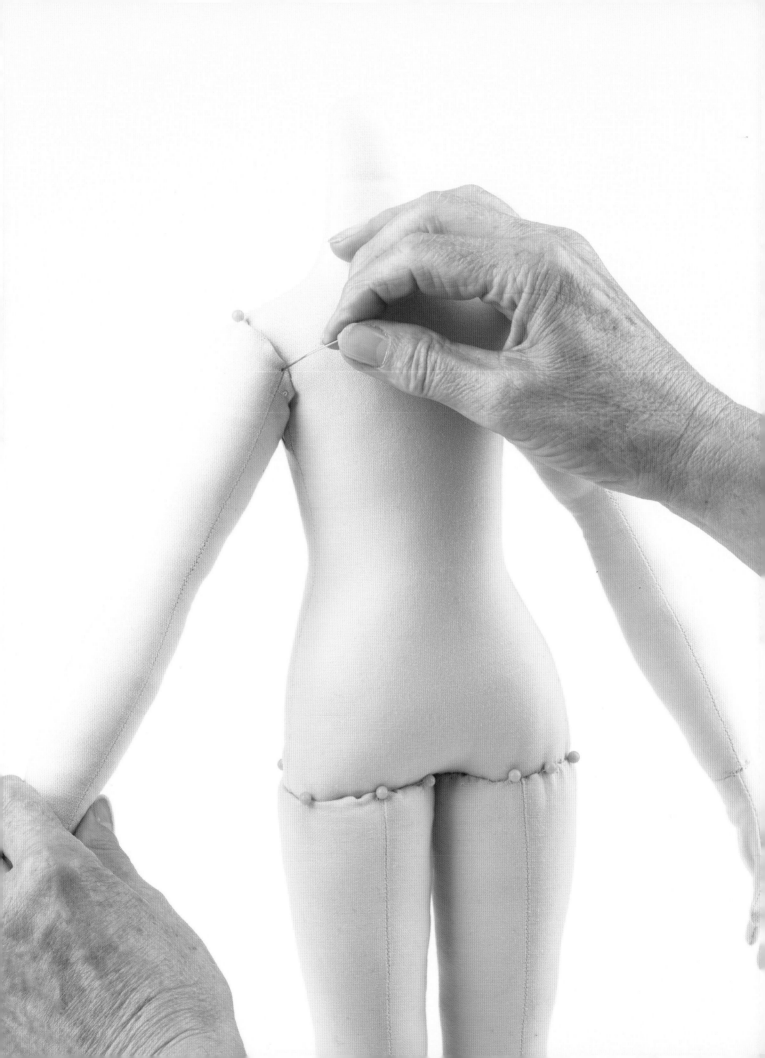

MATERIALS

The materials for faces and general doll making can be found in a good haberdashery department, a craft supply shop or online.

FABRICS

Most doll makers have a particular fabric that they prefer to use, and my advice is to work with what you like but also experiment with something new now and again to push your creative boundaries.

I like to use a good-quality 100 per cent cotton quilting fabric because it has a little give – helping you to mould the head and achieve a nice, smooth finish when the head is stuffed. It can also be bought in a variety of skin tone colours. If you struggle to find the colour you desire, you can easily dye quilting fabric.

Pimatex also works well. It is a finely woven cotton with a high thread count and is good for drawing on.

THREAD

For needle sculpting you need to use a fine strong thread such as polyester quilting thread. For any machine sewing, basic polyester thread is fine. I always use a colour which matches the fabric I am using. This is because, once the head is stitched and stuffed, the stitching may show and look unsightly.

STUFFING

Always use a good-quality polyester toy stuffing; it needs to be soft, light and springy. If the stuffing feels rough and doesn't spring back it is likely to compact into hard balls and make obtaining a good result very difficult.

YARNS

There is an amazing variety of natural and synthetic fibres and yarns that can be used to create the hair for your dolls, and I will go into detail with this on pages 85–87. Anything that is fibrous can be needle felted into the head so try all types of natural wool, silk waste fibres, and even some synthetic fibres.

Wensleydale and Teeswater sheep produce long curly staples, Blueface Leicester have tight little curls and Mohair goats produce long fine curls. Merino tops are carded or processed and will give you a soft continuous yarn which can be teased and arranged into wonderful hair styles.

A variety of silk fibres can be used, but they will require a bit more felting in.

There are many interesting novelty yarns available. These need to be stitched to the head but will produce wild and extravagant hairstyles.

SYNTHETIC HAIR PIECES

One of the most interesting products to use when creating hairstyles for your characters is synthetic hair pieces. These are made in a continuous strip or weft, and come in a huge variety of styles and colours.

TOOLS

Like your materials, the equipment needed for faces and general doll making can be found in a good haberdashery department, a craft supply shop or online.

SEWING KIT

- **SEWING MACHINE** Always keep your sewing machine in good working order and change your needle regularly. A blunt needle will affect the quality of your stitching and may cause snagging. With machine needles, I use size 70 (US 10) for fine fabrics like silk, 80 (US 12) for fabrics like cotton and 90 (US 14) for heavy fabrics. In addition, a clear open foot (see page 104) will make sewing around intricate shapes much easier and is an invaluable asset.
- **HAND-SEWING NEEDLES** For sculpting the faces you will need a long fine darning needle. For sewing together and jointing doll body pieces (see pages 102–117), no. 7 doll needles that are 20.5cm (8in) in length are ideal.
- **THIMBLE** I find this particularly useful when working with thick fabric or when attaching heads and limbs.
- **PINS** I prefer to use good-quality dressmaking pins for general use, and long glass-headed pins for holding heads and limbs in place for stitching.
- **FABRIC SCISSORS** You will need a good, sharp pair of dressmaking shears and a small pair of sharp scissors for intricate work. Always keep your scissors sharp as it will make cutting accurately so much easier. Never use your fabric scissors for cutting paper or wire as you will only blunt them.
- **MEASURING EQUIPMENT** You will need a tape measure, ruler and a seam guide.
- **SEAM SEALANT** An invaluable addition to your kit, this is applied to stop fabric from fraying.
- **IRON** A small travelling iron and an ironing pad are useful if you have them.
- **PAPER SCISSORS** You will need a small and a large pair of paper scissors for cutting out patterns.
- **PENCIL** A propelling pencil has a fine point, good for tracing around patterns accurately.

STUFFING FORK

This special fork, or something similar, will help to push stuffing into heads, bodies and limbs.

FORCEPS OR HAEMOSTATS

It is possible to buy utility/craft versions of these medical instruments, and they really are invaluable pieces of equipment for a doll maker. They are used for turning things inside out and for stuffing. Forceps come in all different shapes and sizes, but I find the 17.75cm (7in) length the most useful.

FINGER-TURNING TOOLS

Invaluable for turning those intricate shapes, such as fingers, inside out. They consist of a metal tube and rod.

FREEZER PAPER

This is a paper with a shiny waxed finish on one side, and is commonly used for making patterns as you can lay the shiny side onto your fabric and iron it to the fabric for easy cutting (see page 105).

ACRYLIC GLOSS GEL

I like to use Glossy Accents™ by Ranger. This clear gloss gel is applied to dried painted features and, when dry, makes lips, eyes and nails look shiny.

GLUE

PVA glue is a useful addition to your kit, and is ideal for attaching eyelashes and eyelids. However, it should be applied sparingly and with a cocktail stick or something similar. This is because, while it dries clear, it can create hard edges if too much is applied.

PLIERS

You will need a pair of 17.75cm (7in) pliers for cutting armature wire, and a pair of 10cm (4in) pliers for snipping into smaller items such as pipe cleaners/chenille stems.

ARMATURE WIRE

This is made of aluminium, which is pliable and easy to manipulate. It is used by sculptors to make a supportive framework for their sculptures, and can be used in the same way for cloth doll making to make a hidden structure inside the dolls. I mostly use a 4mm (3/16in) thick wire.

PIPER CLEANER/CHENILLE STEM

Similar to the armature wire, this is used as a supportive structure for smaller body pieces such as ears and hands.

NEEDLE-FELTING NEEDLE

The end of this needle has double barbs, which enables you to push fibres such as wool or silk into the small weave of fabric, to create the hair for your doll.

DRAWING & COLOURING EQUIPMENT

There are different techniques and media for drawing and painting faces but I mainly use soft colouring pencils (such as those by Derwent), acrylic paint and waterproof/fade-proof pens. However, you can use your favourite medium to develop the ideas presented in this book.

PENCILS

Use soft colouring pencils. It doesn't matter what make they are, so long as they blend together with ease. Use a sharp pencil for detail and for defining shapes and the side of the pencil for softer shading.

When shading any area, always use more than one colour as this will give depth and dimension to your work. For example, ochre and terracotta blend together to make a good flesh tone.

Some good, basic colours to have in your kit would be:
- **FLESH TONES** Yellow ochre, burnt ochre, sienna brown and dark umber.
- **AT LEAST TWO CORRESPONDING SHADES OF ANY OTHER COLOUR** For example, scarlet and magenta, apple green and dark green, true blue and Prussian blue.

TIP

Keep a scrap of fabric handy for testing colours rather than working straight on to the face.

FABRIC ERASER

This will erase light-coloured pencil marks but not very dark colours.

WATERPROOF/FADE-PROOF PENS

These are mainly used for the eyes, pupils, eyelashes and eyebrows. They come in different thicknesses, 1 to 3 being the most useful. I mostly use black, brown and red, but they come in a wide range of other colours. They should be waterproof/fade-proof as indicated but it is always a good idea to test them on a scrap of fabric in case they bleed.

STENCILS

Small-scale stencils are excellent for applying pattern and texture to the face.

GEL PENS

Readily available from retailers, they come in many colours, some with sparkle or metallic finish. They have thicker points than waterproof/fade-proof pens, so they are good for decoration but not for fine detail. As with waterproof/fade-proof pens, always test them first for colour and bleeding.

FINE PAINT BRUSHES

I tend to use sizes 2 and 4.

ACRYLIC PAINT

I use white acrylic for painting the eyes and highlights. Metallic acrylic paint can also be used for decorative effects and finishes.

ACRYLIC FIXATIVE SPRAY

This will seal the colour and stop it smudging or fading. Always read the instructions on the tin carefully and use outside or in a well ventilated room. They are not recommended for those with respiratory problems.

NAIL VARNISH

Always test nail varnish on a scrap of fabric before using it on your finished doll. It can be used on the fingers or lips of a doll, but should be applied with a small, fine brush – not the brush that comes with the nail varnish.

OTHER ESSENTIALS:
- **TOOTH PICK**
- **ERASER**
- **SHARPENER**

Inspiration
& design

INFLUENCES, SOURCES & STYLES

'People often ask me where I get the inspiration for my dolls, and the simple answer is from anywhere and everywhere.'

I could be flicking through a magazine and a picture or advert will catch my eye, or I could be walking down the street and see somebody who might inspire a doll. Sometimes I will be actively looking for ideas and sometimes they will just jump out at me.

One of the reasons for writing this book was to encourage people to look at and explore as many different art forms and cultures as possible, as a way of finding inspiration and stimuli for designing unique cloth dolls. This is known as creating source materials, as these will be references you use throughout your doll making to create your chosen subject. Source materials need to be stored and recorded in some way. I keep a series of scrap books. They're nothing fancy – they contain cuttings from magazines, postcards, photographs and sketches with notes. Essentially anything, really, that takes my liking. It's useful to keep them in subject order: History, Fashion, Dance, Faces, Theatre and so on.

You can't just sit down with a blank piece of fabric and a pencil and expect to create a face. A point of reference is invaluable, and that is where all your source materials come into play.

PORTRAITS

Portraits – painted or otherwise – are the most obvious starting point, and I encourage you to look at anything from the earliest examples made in history to modern-day creations. For simple drawn faces, early icons, frescos and Byzantine art provide basic but effective facial images, and painters such as Modigliani, Picasso, Matisse and Erté have all created wonderful facial expressions using simple line drawings.

There are many artists, past and present, to refer to when looking for inspiration for drawing realistic faces. Both Albrecht Dürer, a German Renaissance artist, and Lucian Freud, a twentieth-century British artist, are renowned for their draughtmanship in portraiture. Sandro Botticelli, the early Italian Renaissance artist, is known for perfect proportions and clarity of line in his figurative paintings. I particularly like the serene quality in the faces he depicts. Paul Gauguin experimented with colour in the French Impressionist style, triggered by his time in Tahiti, and he often painted bright, glowing portraits of Tahitian women. The Art Deco portraits of Tamara de Lempicka, and the geometric abstractions of Modernist Wyndham Lewis's portraits both show highly stylized faces with bold shapes and strong lines. Finally, Dame Laura Knight's strong Impressionist style captured the essence of the people, and the characters they adopted, of those in the entertainment industry, of working-class individuals or those outside traditional society – from circus performers and ballet dancers to factory workers during World War Two and Travellers.

You can find portraits in books or on the internet, but if you get the chance, visit your local art gallery or even your local town hall to look at any portraits there. You will find seeing the real thing in the flesh will have more depth, dimension and colour than images captured and displayed in books or digitally.

SCULPTURES

Sculptures also provide a good point of reference, especially as their three-dimensional format relates well to a doll face. I like church effigies with their serene expressions and – by contrast – those impish or grotesque gargoyles! Again, look at sculptures across history, from Classical and Medieval periods through to the modern day – in the latter group, I particularly admire sculptors such as Constantin Brâncuşi, Modigliani and Mirsad Begić.

CROSS-CULTURAL INFLUENCES

You will never be short of inspiration if you look at any traditional art or sculpture from other civilizations and cultures. Think of the strong, bold features of ancient African art and sculptures, the decorative masks and tattoos of the Maori people, the beautiful faces of the Cambodian and Indian goddesses, and the ancient stone carvings of the Aztec and Mayan peoples.

HIGH FASHION

This is among my favourite sources of inspiration. All the big names in fashion produce amazing shows every year, throughout the seasons, and use fantastic fabrics, accessories and, of course, make-up and hair. I find Vivienne Westwood, John Galliano, Thierry Mugler and the late Alexander McQueen particularly inspirational.

THEATRE & FILM

My other favourite source of stimuli, theatre and film can provide a more diverse and flamboyant style for your dolls, from costumes to make-up and hairstyles. They are particularly useful sources to turn to when designing a face, from fantasy fairies to aliens. There are many places you can find these sources – from stills of the films themselves to dedicated websites, books and costume galleries.

DEVELOPING A DESIGN

'Once you have decided on a subject or theme for your doll, do as much research and collect and record as much visual information as possible. Recording your source material in some way will help you to focus your ideas and develop an original design.'

I prefer to do a series of sketches when developing a new design, as I find that drawing really makes me look at a subject and get an understanding of shape, form and texture. Then I jot a few notes afterwards to help me remember any additional details.

Many people find the thought of drawing quite daunting, but remember these sketches are for your own reference and not for an art exhibition. They will help you take ideas from inside your head and develop a two-dimensional image into a three-dimensional doll. If this method doesn't suit you, you could make up a collage from photos and photocopied images or compile a library of pictures on your tablet.

Start to pick out your favourite elements from your research. You may take a face from one source and a hairstyle from another. Also use this principle when designing the costume: take a sleeve, a drape or a decorative effect from one source and put it together with another to create an original design.

Remember to use your source material as inspiration only to develop an idea. Do not copy an image outright, as this may infringe copyright laws.

Creating sketches and collages

This is a collage I created, based on statues, wall carvings and paintings of goddesses I saw in Vietnam. I have used one of my photographs as a central image, and also photocopies of other images I took on the same trip. Drawing figures, faces and patterns helps me to clarify my designs. Finally, I painted in a colour palette that evokes the rich textiles I saw in the country, which I found so inspiring.

Designing & colouring a face

For many people the thought of drawing a face puts them in a nervous spin, but if you look at each component part separately – eyes, nose and mouth – and break them down into a series of lines, curves and circles, creating a face isn't as complicated or as scary as you might imagine.

Take your time. This not a job to rush and it is much more enjoyable when you can relax; you can't knock up a face while you are waiting for the potatoes to boil.

Try to practise on a scrap piece of fabric first. Don't be tempted to work straight on to the head. I also recommend practising drawing the features of a face on a much larger scale to your finished head; you will become more aware of the processes involved, and will be more confident when you do it on the smaller finished head. In addition, practising on scrap fabric means you can experiment and change things as you go along. I always make at least three heads for each doll and then choose the one I like best.

PROPORTIONS OF THE FACE

There are various formulas for drawing the proportions of a face, some of which can be quite complicated. I prefer to keep things as simple as possible, so try this method first.

1 Draw a vertical line down the centre of the oval that forms the face.

2 EYE Draw a horizontal line at the head's halfway point. Mark the eyes along this line.

3 NOSE Draw a horizontal line halfway between the eye line and the chin. Mark the base of the nose over the line, then draw in the remaining nose details above this.

4 MOUTH Draw a horizontal line halfway between the nose and the chin. This is where the lips meet.

This basic formula is a good starting point for drawing a face. However, if you always follow this, you do run the risk of producing a similar face each time. So, once you are confident with this method, I encourage you to get creative and start breaking some of those rules.

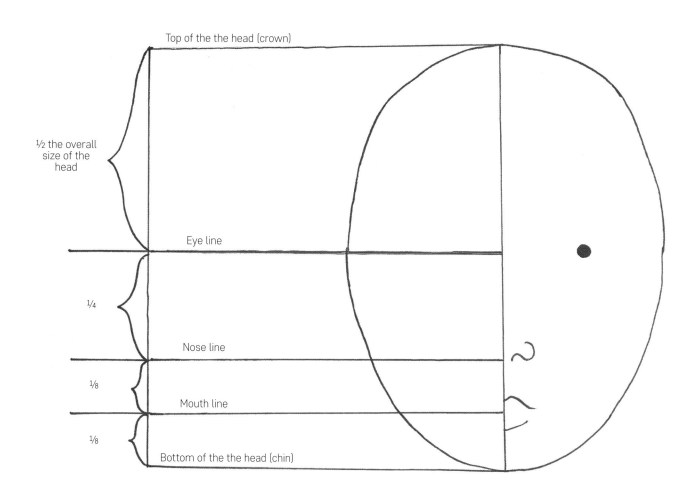

Top of the the head (crown)

½ the overall size of the head

Eye line

¼

Nose line

⅛

Mouth line

⅛

Bottom of the the head (chin)

Now your source materials, observations and imagination will come into play. You will start to notice all the different features and the variations that make up a face and the way that they create unique and individual characters.

The shape of the face is also an important factor. Throughout the book I will be focusing on Long, Square and Oval faces (see also pages 42–52), and have provided templates for these at the back of the book (see pages 118–129) but there are other shapes you could explore.

It is not just the shape of the face you need to consider, but also the placement of the features. Note the specific differences in:

- the position of the eyes
- the distance between the eyes and the nose
- the distance between the nose and the mouth
- the distance between the mouth and the chin
- the variation in size and shape of the eyes, mouth, nose and eyebrows.

These four faces are all the same shape but look like different characters because the position and shape of the features vary.

25

DRAWING EYES

The basic technique

To achieve a good three-dimensional effect, use and blend several tones of one colour, and use at least two or three colours together. This will help you to achieve depth and dimension. For this eye demonstration I have used grass green and peacock green for the iris, and ochre, terracotta and dark green for the eyelid.

You will already have marked out the eye position when you planned the face (see page 24), so let's take it from there.

Swatch of eye colours

Top
Eyelid colours: dark green, terracotta and ochre.

Bottom
Iris colours: peacock green and grass green.

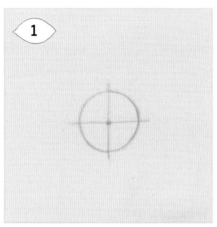
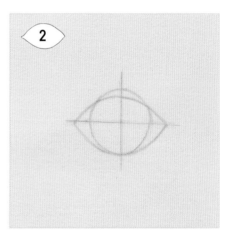
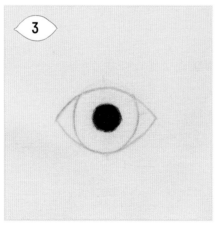
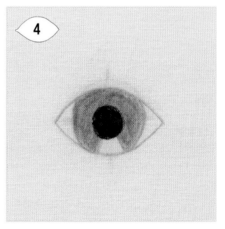

1 Using a coloured pencil close to the colour of the fabric (here, I have used ochre), draw a circle for the iris around the eye position you marked when planning the face.

2 Draw a curved line which cuts off the top of the iris and then a curved line which skims the bottom of the iris.

3 Using a black waterproof/fade-proof pen, enlarge the pupil.

4 Colour the main area of the iris in the palest shade in your selection of pencils, leaving a section at the bottom uncoloured.

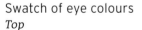

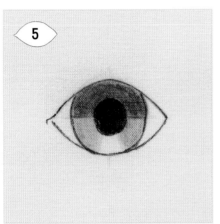

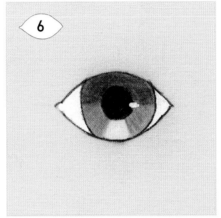

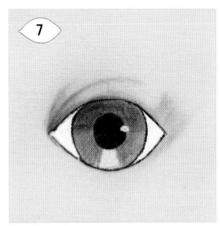

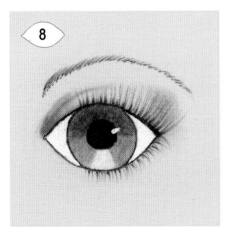

5 Colour the top part of the iris in the darkest pencil colour, then outline the iris and the top and bottom of the eyelids with the black waterproof pen.

6 Using white acrylic paint and a small brush, paint the whites of the eyes. Wipe the brush on a tissue to remove some of the paint – this will give you a paler shade of white with which to paint the remaining bottom section of the iris. Finish by putting a white highlight dot on the edge of the pupil. The dot should be on the same side on each eye – i.e. both on the left or both on the right.

7 Draw a curved line for the eyelid and then shade along the socket line and at the inner and outer corners.

8 Use a fine black pen and a flicking motion to draw several rows of eyelashes. They should ALWAYS flick outwards towards the sides of the face and should also finish at the inner edge of the pupil; they should not go right to the inner eye corners. Draw in the eyebrows with a flesh-coloured pencil, then draw in several rows of small lines with a black pen.

By practising drawing eyes on a larger scale, you will become familiar with the shapes and process; this will give you more confidence when drawing on a smaller scale, on the head of your doll.

Once you have tried these basic principles you will be able to use your source material to build on this key shape to create an amazing variety of wonderful eyes.

Changing expressions

By changing the position of the pupil, you can create different expressions.

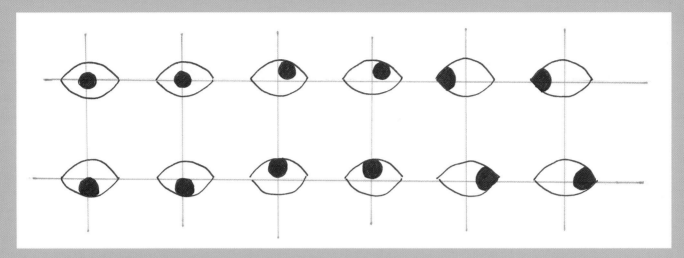

You can also change the expression of your doll's face by altering the size and position of the pupil and iris.

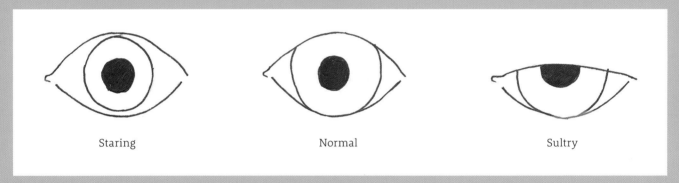

Staring   Normal   Sultry

Combine both of these to create different eye shapes.

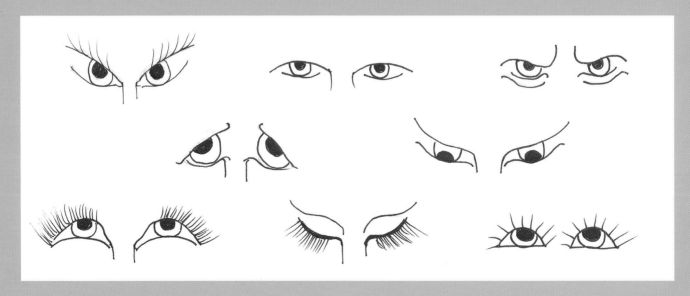

EYEBROWS

Although eyes are a very important feature of the face, the eyebrows provide a lot of expression. Their shape and placement as well as the distance from the eye can determine character. Drawing the eyebrow for realistic eyes is simple – using a flesh-coloured pencil, draw in your chosen eyebrow shape. Then, with a fine black pen and starting at the inner eye edge, draw a row of several small lines that follow the direction of your eyebrow shape. Some of the more stylized eyebrows are achieved with solid black lines.

Gallery of simple line eyes

It is possible to create a face by using simple lines. If you look at artists like Erté, Modigliani, Matisse and Picasso, you will discover how effective a few simple lines can be, and how many variations are possible.

This technique is most effective on flat faces. I have included galleries of eyes, noses and mouths drawn with simple lines throughout the first half of this book; have fun mixing and matching to create your own doll.

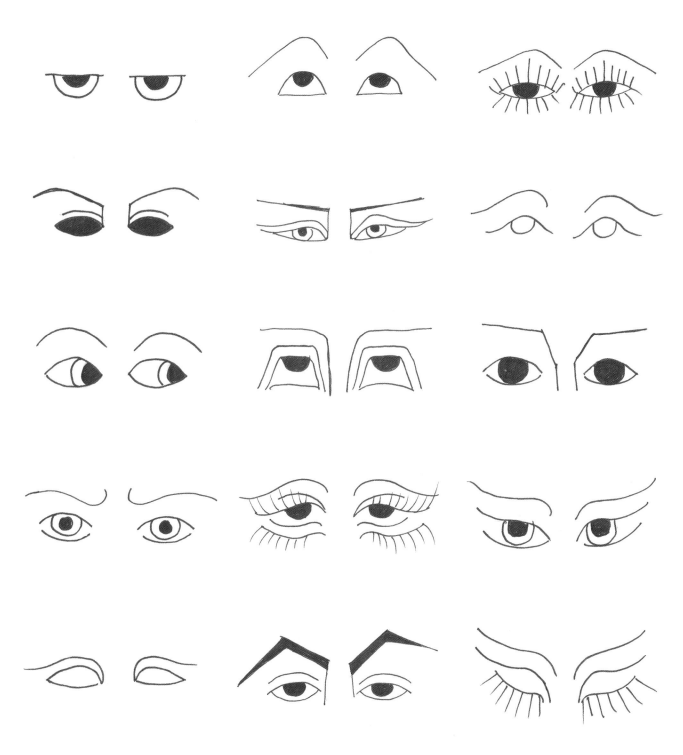

GALLERY OF SIMPLE LINE EYES ON FABRIC

These line drawings are influenced by the avant-garde art movements in the early twentieth century, but you could experiment with other shapes for your own dolls.

Gallery of realistic eyes

I developed these more realistic eyes by looking at portraits by various artists, as well as photographs or images in magazines. Look at the basic structures and shapes of the eye (see also pages 26–29) then use these to experiment. Pay particular attention to:

- the shape of the eye
- the position of the pupil
- the style and depth of the eyelid
- the shape, curve and depth of the eyebrows.

By combining all these elements, you can create a wide range of expressions.

Feel free to experiment with your eye colours! If you are new to designing eyes, start off with a few shades of one colour, such as green, as described on page 26. When you are feeling more confident, you can introduce other colours such as terractotta or grey into the mix to give greater depth and realism.

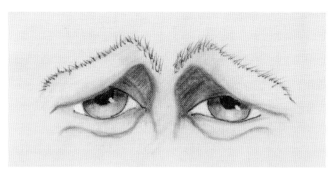
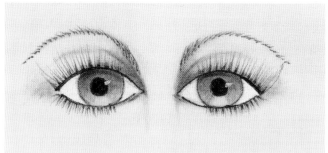

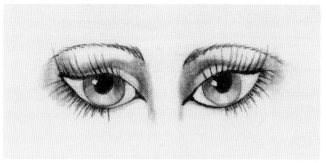
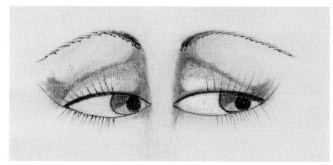

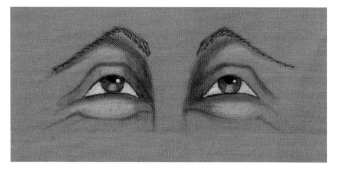
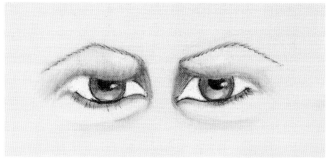

Gallery of decorative eyes

Once again, I looked at my source material for inspiration for creating my decorative faces. I always find facial decoration from different cultures, art, film and fantasy makeup and natural elements very inspirational.

DRAWING NOSES

Creating simple line noses

As described before, inspirational sources that portray faces in an abstract way are invaluable for giving you ideas for noses made from simple outlines.

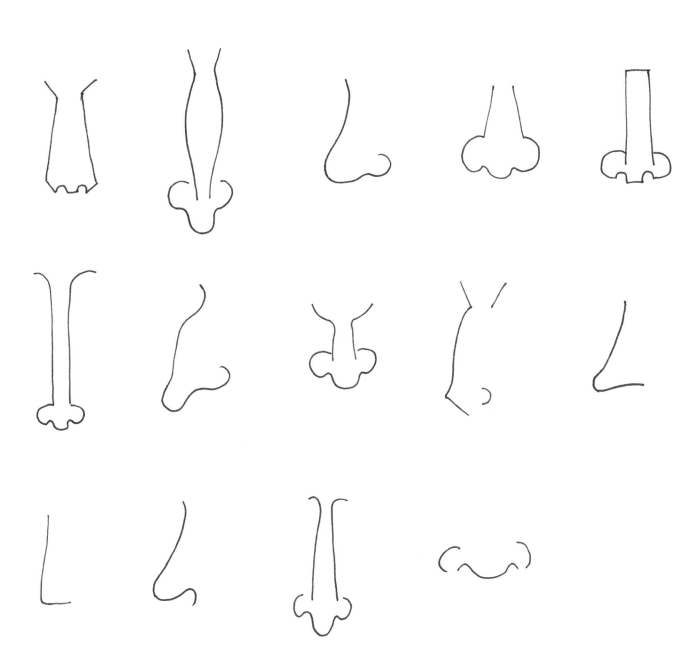

Creating realistic noses

THE BASIC TECHNIQUE

To draw a realistic nose, you just need to break it down into its component parts – these are simple shapes consisting of circles, ovals and straight lines. Shading is also an important part of the process, as it will give depth and dimension to this important feature.

When choosing your soft colouring pencils select mid-tones – such as ochre – to fill in the basic areas, darker tones such as terracotta and raw umber to create depth, and then white for highlights.

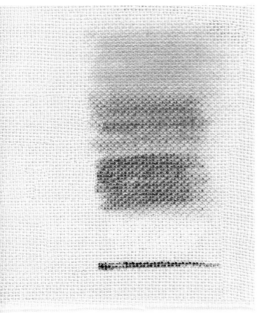

Swatch of typical colours for shading the nose.

Top to bottom: ochre, terracotta, raw umber, white and brown.

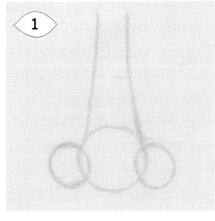

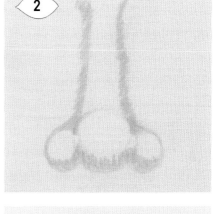

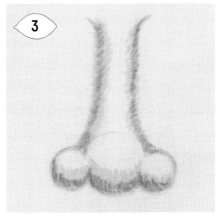

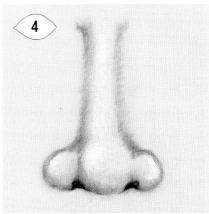

1 With an ochre-coloured pencil, draw a central circle and then two smaller circles on either side that slightly overlap. Draw in the bridge of the nose, ensuring that it is narrower at the top then gradually widens outwards as it touches the large central circle.

2 Use the ochre-coloured pencil once again to shade down each side of the bridge of the nose and along the bottom of the circles.

3 Switch to the terracotta-coloured pencil and shade just outside the same areas.

4 Use the raw umber pencil to darken the areas around the nose wings, then switch to the brown pencil to accentuate the nostrils. Finally, add white highlights down the bridge of the nose, the tip of the nose and nose wings – make these highlights slightly off centre, for realism. To finish, blend the darker shades together, and soften the white highlight, by gently rubbing them with a piece of cloth.

Gallery of realistic noses

After you have practised the basic technique for creating a nose, you can explore the many variations. Consider the length and width of the bridge of the nose, as well as the size and shape of the nostrils.

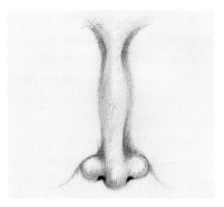

Ochre
Raw umber
Sepia
Peach
White

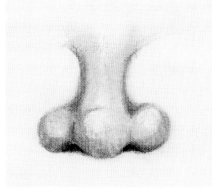

Ochre
Raw umber
Peach
Burnt umber
White

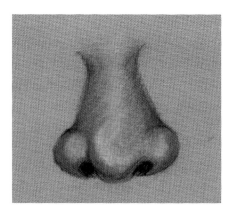

Terracotta
Raw umber
Brown earth
White
Sepia

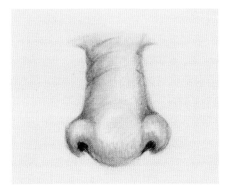

Ochre
Sepia
Raw umber
White

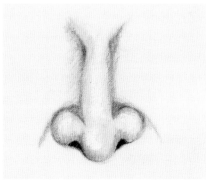

Ochre
Raw umber
Sepia
Peach
White

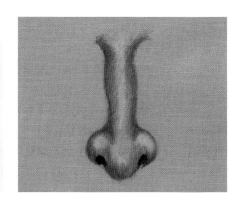

Ochre
Terracotta
Raw umber
Sepia
White

DRAWING MOUTHS

The basic technique

In general, women have fuller lips than men, who tend to have thinner, wider mouths. There are, however, always exceptions to the rule, so it is worth noting variances by looking closely at real people and at your source materials. I usually base my mouths on those seen in magazines, paintings and sculptures, as it allows me to study the shapes longer.

When it comes to drawing the mouth, think of the lips as a series of large and small ovals and circles. Using different combinations and arrangements of these will produce different shaped mouths.

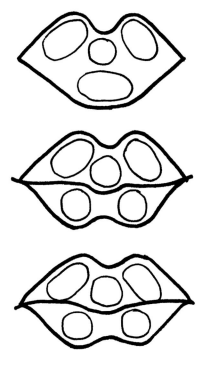

Start by drawing a combination of ovals and circles. This will give you a guide for the mouth outline. I tend to draw two to three circles or ovals for the upper lip, then just one or two for the lower lip.

Then, draw an outline around these shapes to define the mouth – the circles and ovals will influence and help shape the outline.

When you draw the centre line, you can decide whether you draw the ends of the line upwards to create a smiling mouth, or the ends downwards to create a sad mouth.

Note how, in the examples above, using a different arrangement of ovals and circles affects the shape of the mouth outline – here, specifically, the lower lip outline.

Colouring a closed mouth

By using pencils in several shades of red then blending the colours together, you will create depth and dimension to the lips.

1 Begin by colouring both lips with the main colour.

2 Layer a darker shade lightly over the top of the upper lip for extra definition.

3 Using the dark pencil once again, or a red pen, outline the top bow of the lip, the centre part of the lower lip and the centre line. Try not to outline the whole mouth as it will make it look too harsh.

4 Finally, use a darker pencil or brown pen to add some contour lines to the top and bottom of the centre line.

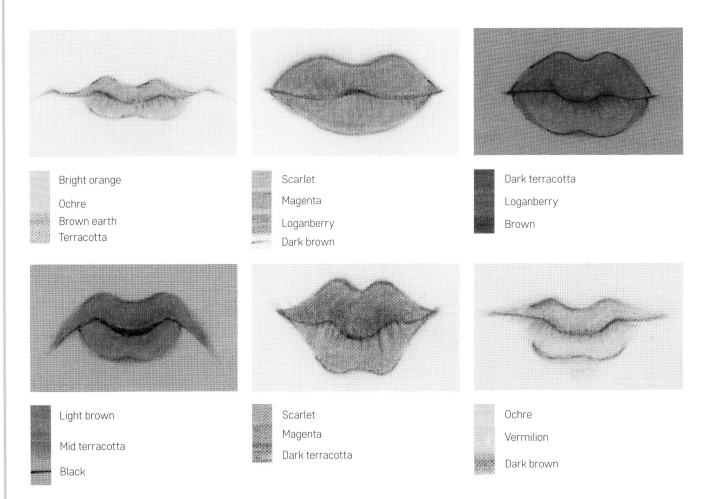

Bright orange
Ochre
Brown earth
Terracotta

Scarlet
Magenta
Loganberry
Dark brown

Dark terracotta
Loganberry
Brown

Light brown
Mid terracotta
Black

Scarlet
Magenta
Dark terracotta

Ochre
Vermilion
Dark brown

Ochre
Vermilion
Mid terracotta
Dark brown

Tip

To create the impression of lips with red lipstick, I recommend using base colours like scarlet and magenta, with darker shading such as mahogany red and Tuscan red. For more natural colouring, use vermilion, orange, ochre and terracotta.

Colouring an open mouth

There are a few points to consider when drawing and colouring an open mouth. Depending on the angle you are looking at, the teeth can appear either concave or convex. The average number of teeth in an adult's mouth is 32, but we should apply the rule 'less is more' to represent them, rather than worrying about the actual number. You may only need about six teeth on the top to make the mouth look realistic. If you make them too small and try to cram too many in, they start to look a bit vampirish.

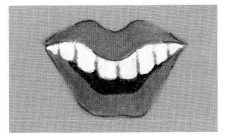

 Terracotta

Ochre

Dark terracotta

Scarlet

Magenta

Loganberry

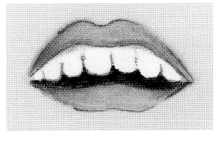

 Ochre

Orange

Terracotta

 Scarlet

Magenta

Loganberry

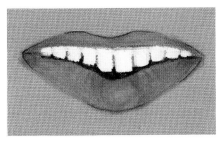

Terracotta

Ochre

Dark terracotta

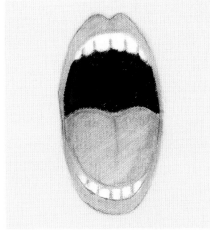

Vermilion

Scarlet

Blush

Terracotta

1 Begin by colouring the lips as described opposite.

2 Using an ochre pencil, start by drawing the first two teeth either side of the centre-line of the head (see page 24) and work outwards. This will ensure that you don't end up with a tooth in the centre.

3 Draw the desired number of teeth – remember to not cram in too many teeth; about six to eight along the top and bottom is perfect.

3 Use white acrylic paint to paint in the individual teeth, leaving a slight gap between each tooth.

4 Outline the lower part of the teeth with a grey or dark brown pen.

5 Finish by colouring in the mouth opening with the black waterproof pen.

SHADING A REALISTIC FACE

By studying faces from magazines, paintings, photographs and other source materials, you will have noticed how faces vary in shape and structure. Many of these differences can be achieved through shading. When it comes to doll making, I like to shade in the faces after the main features – eyes, nose and mouth – have been added. To shade, use the side of the pencil for soft shading and the point for details.

Paler skin tones

Fabrics for paler skin tones can vary enormously, from cream to pale peach, so take some time to choose the colour that suits your character. To create skin tones use soft colouring pencils in shades such as ochre, terracotta, peach, red, orange, and white or cream.

1 With the side of an ochre pencil, shade down the side of the nose, the outside edge of each nose wing, the top of the forehead, the sides of the face, and under the lower lip.

2 Now use terracotta to shade the same areas, but don't quite cover up the ochre.

3 Use two shades of red or peach to colour the cheek area.

4 Finally, use white or cream to highlight the bridge of the nose, the centre of each nose wing, and the tip of the nose.

The shading may look harsh at this stage, but when everything is blended together it will produce subtle tones.

The right side of the face has only been shaded with an ochre pencil; the left side has been shaded with darker terracotta around the edge, with red shading on the cheeks.

Use a piece of fabric and rub it gently on the face to blend the colours together. If you think it is too pale, you can always add extra colour and then blend again.

An older man

When looking for source materials for older faces, you may find books and websites on stage make-up invaluable as particular techniques are used to exaggerate wrinkles and contours. It is also important to consider hair and hairstyles; I had this rather coarse, wavy fleece that was just right for creating the bushy eyebrows and moustache of this dapper old gent.

40

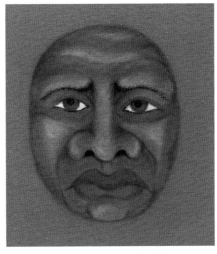

The left side of the face shows the first stage of shading the face, with white or cream added to certain areas for highlights. The right side shows the added darker shading, including ochre, terracotta, dark brown and black.

When you have completed all the shading on both sides of the face, blend the colours together with a piece of cloth. Then, draw or shade in the remaining facial details – eyebrows, eyes, nostrils and mouth.

Darker skin tones

You can find fabrics that vary from golden brown to really dark brown for dolls with darker skin tones.

1 Start by creating the highlights as these areas are the most dominant. Highlight the bridge of the nose, the cheeks, the forehead, the chin, the end of the nose and the nose wings with white or cream.

2 Use mid-tones such as ochre and terracotta to shade the side of the bridge of the nose, the eye sockets, the forehead, down the sides of the face and under the lips.

3 Finally, use dark brown and black to add depth and definition to the forehead, sides of the face, eye sockets, bridge of the nose and nose wings.

Older faces

There are obviously more lines on an older face, and these lines should follow the natural contours of the face to create credible folds and wrinkles. Straight lines will not give the desired three-dimensional effect, so try to curve the lines gently across the different areas of the face.

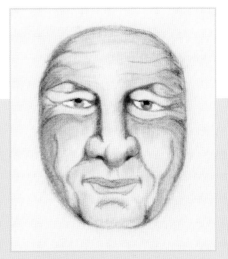

1 Plan out the face in the usual way and then add the age lines following the contours of the face.

2 With an ochre pencil shade all around the side of the face, sides of the bridge of the nose, cheeks, chin and under the nose. Use a terracotta pencil to go over all these areas and then use white or cream to highlight the centre of the bridge of the nose, the tip and nostrils, the cheeks and forehead.

3 Finally add extra detailing with a dark brown pencil. Shade the side of the face following the contours, down each side of the bridge of the nose and the eye sockets. Add any line details to give definition to the face.

GALLERY OF SIMPLE LINE FACES

Long faces

Templates for tracing are on pages 118 and 119.

Simple long face #1

Simple long face #2

Simple long face #3

Simple long face #4

Simple long face #5

Flat faces rely on drawn lines to develop their features and characteristics, unlike dimensional faces where the shape and position of the features is dictated by the pattern.

You will need to consider the placement of the eyes, nose and mouth for your flat face much more carefully; however, this does give you more possibilities to develop a wider variety of faces.

I have used three different-shaped heads – long, square and oval – throughout this section, which will enable you to mix and match the features for your own doll.

Square faces

Templates for tracing are on pages 119 and 120.

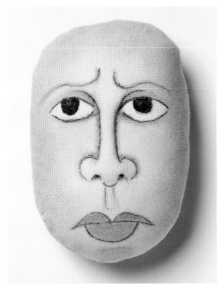

Simple square face #1

Simple square face #2

Simple square face #3

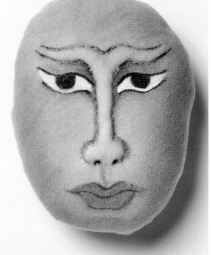

Simple square face #4

Simple square face #5

Oval faces

Templates for tracing are on pages 120 and 121.

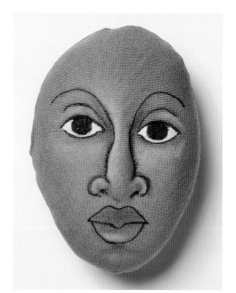

Simple oval face #1

Simple oval face #2

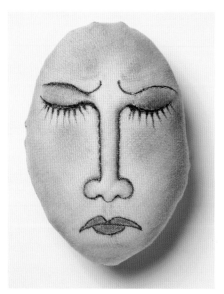

Simple oval face #3

Simple oval face #4

Simple oval face #5

GALLERY OF REALISTIC FACES

Drawing a realistic face is perhaps the most difficult technique to master, as you are considering not just the placement of the eyes, nose and lips, but the lines, contours and shading of the face. Once again, painted portraits were invaluable sources when creating these faces, but I also amassed a collection of pictures from magazines which were particular useful for facial expressions.

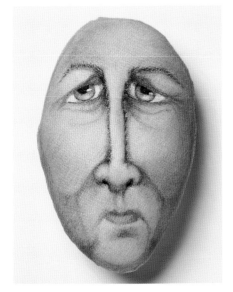

Realistic long face #1

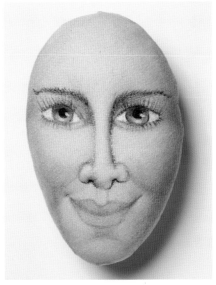

Realistic long face #2

Long faces
Templates for tracing are on pages 122 and 123.

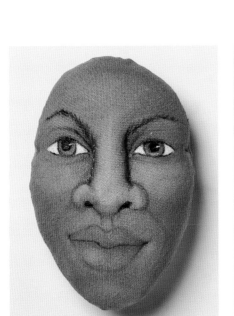

Realistic long face #3

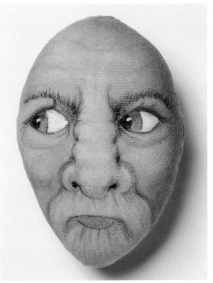

Realistic long face #4

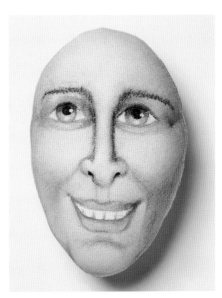

Realistic long face #5

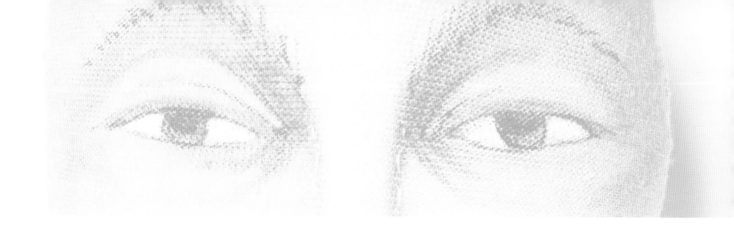

Square faces

Templates for tracing are on pages 123 and 124.

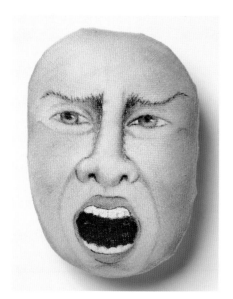

Realistic square face #1

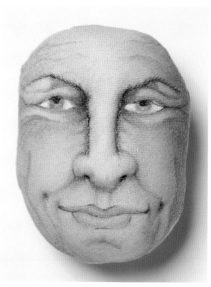

Realistic square face #2

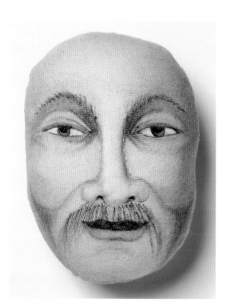

Realistic square face #3

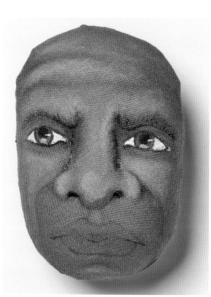

Realistic square face #4

Oval faces

Templates for tracing are on pages 124 and 125.

Realistic oval face #1

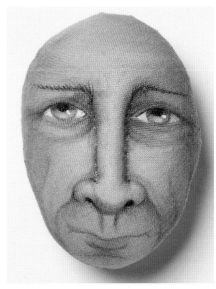

Realistic oval face #2

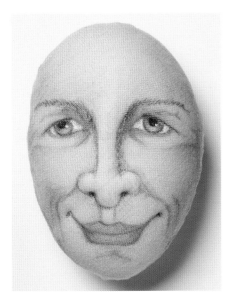

Realistic oval face #3

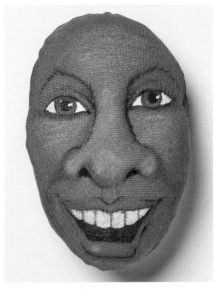

Realistic oval face #4

Realistic oval face #5

Dimensional faces

Drawing and colouring a dimensional face (see page 68) is very similar to drawing and colouring a flat face, except the position of the nose and mouth has already been determined by the pattern. You will only need to mark in the position of the eyes (see page 24). Once you have done this, just follow the techniques for colouring the eyes (see page 26), shading the nose (see page 35), drawing and colouring the mouth (see page 38) and shading the face (see page 40).

I have provided three different head patterns with different profiles (see pages 132 and 133), which you can use to create different characters.

Use the information on the proportions of the face (see page 24) to help you; there is also further guidance on marking out a dimensional face later, on page 70.

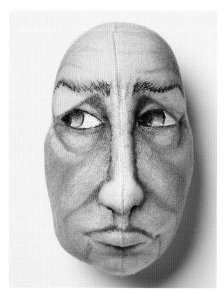
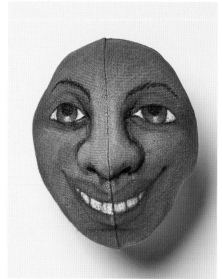
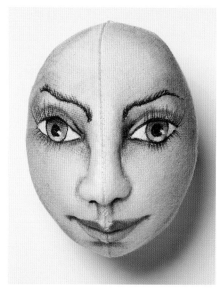

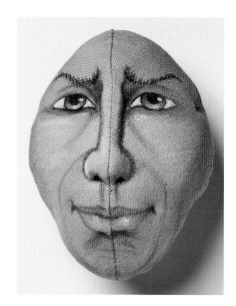

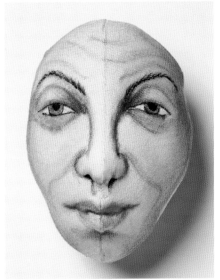
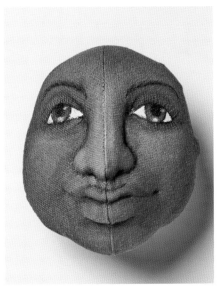

GALLERY OF DECORATIVE FACES

Long faces

Templates for tracing are on pages 125 and 126.

Decorative long face #1

Decorative long face #2

Decorative long face #3

Decorative long face #4

Decorative long face #5

I find the techniques for creating these faces the most exciting, because the source material is seemingly endless. I have used various cultural influences, fantasy references and designs inspired by nature. Decorative faces enable you to explore and use different mediums and colours, such as acrylic paint, pearlescent or metallic paint, coloured pens – in fact, anything that won't bleed or smudge on fabric. If you're ever unsure, always test on a scrap piece of the same fabric that you'll use for your doll. You can also use small stencils to add patterns and textures.

Square faces

Templates for tracing are on pages 126 and 127.

Decorative square face #1

Decorative square face #2

Decorative square face #3

Decorative square face #4

Decorative square face #5

Oval faces

Templates for tracing are on pages 128 and 129.

Decorative oval face #1

Decorative oval face #2

Decorative oval face #3

Decorative oval face #4

Decorative oval face #5

DESIGNING A COLLAGE FACE

This is a fun technique that lends itself to creating amusing little characters. I use cartoons and caricatures, tribal artwork and medieval sculptures as inspiration. Instead of using pencils or paint, colour and patterns are created through printed cotton fabrics – and not just for the faces, but for the dolls' accessories, hair and costumes, too.

Gallery of collage faces

Collage face #1

Template for tracing is on page 129. Note that I have extended some of main features in the sewn design for effect.

Collage face #2

Template for tracing is on page 129.

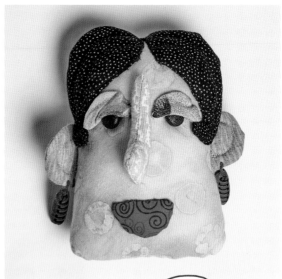

Alternative design

Collage face #3

Template for tracing is on page 130.

Alternative design

Collage face #4

Template for tracing is on page 130.

Alternative design

Collage face #5

Template for tracing is on page 131.

Alternative design

Collage face #6

Template for tracing is on page 131.

Alternative design

Face-making techniques

I have used three techniques for making the faces in this book. They are all very different, and will enable you to produce a variety of exciting and creative faces. Although a flat face has only a two-piece pattern, it is a perfect vehicle for exploring lots of decorative options to create unique faces.

The dimensional face is probably the most versatile of all the techniques, as there are many, many variations that can be made from the four-piece pattern, and it is the pattern that determines the profile and shape of the face. The needle sculpting on the dimensional face is more detailed, and therefore the features are more pronounced.

For the collage face, we will explore the different shapes of the noses, lips and eyes, and then reproduce them in a three-dimensional form using many different, colourful fabrics.

MAKING A FLAT HEAD

Although making a flat face uses simple techniques, it can be tricky to get the stuffing to sit evenly inside. Make sure the head is stuffed firmly and the stuffing is pushed well up to the seams, all the way around. For clarity, I have used a darker thread in these steps. For your own doll, use a thread that matches the colour of the fabric. The square flat face template on page 132 has been used below.

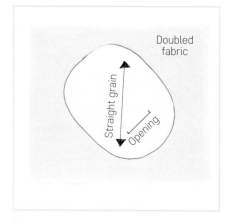

1 Iron the freezer paper pattern onto doubled fabric placed right sides together (see the freezer paper method on page 105), making sure the straight grain line is parallel with the straight grain of the fabric. Sew all the way around the head, using a small 1.5mm stitch on your machine.

2 Cut out the head, adding a 4mm (just over ⅛in) seam allowance all around.

3 Cut a 2.5cm (1in) slit in one layer of the fabric, then turn the head through the slit so that it is right side out. Push out the seam of the head by inserting forceps or a chopstick through the slits and running it around the seam – this will give the head a good shape, ready for stuffing.

4 Stuff the head firmly with stuffing – you can always add more when attaching the head to the body later.

5 Close the opening with temporary stitches or pins, taking the needle from one side of the slit to the other. These contain the stuffing while you draw the face and sculpt the head, and will be removed later when the head is sewn to the body.

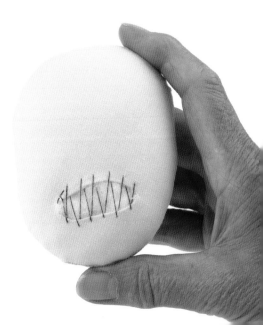

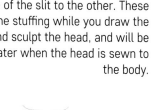

NEEDLE SCULPTING A FLAT FACE

In essence, needle sculpting is drawing thread through the stuffed head in different directions – and in different sections of the head – to pull in the fabric, adding further shape and creating a realistic human profile.

Predominantly, dimensional faces require the most needle sculpting (see pages 70–74). However, even a flat face can be enhanced with a bit of needle sculpting, as this will give it a touch more depth and definition.

When needle sculpting, your stitches should be small enough so that they will not show, but not too small or they will pull through the fabric. Each stitch should be pulled firmly to create the features; however, take care not to pull the thread too tightly or the features will become puckered and distorted. You may find some areas of the face will need to be stitched twice to ensure they hold their shape.

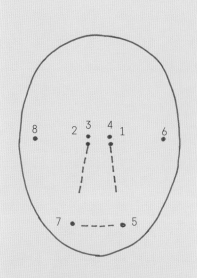

Main sections of a flat face to needle sculpt

1–4 = Inner eye and nose bridge

5–8 = Cheeks

Marking out and drawing the face

Unlike the dimensional face, I tend to needle sculpt flat faces after I have drawn and coloured in the face, as the design influences the placement of the stitches.

Before drawing, you will need to mark in the positions of the key features to ensure you needle sculpt correctly. For flat faces, marking the positions of the features prior to drawing and colouring is essential, to ensure the facial features are not irregular or disproportionate.

To mark out the key features on your doll's face, select a coloured pencil in a medium tone, such as ochre. Then, using the information on Proportions of the Face on page 24 to help you, mark out the vertical and horizontal lines on the face, and draw in the basic shapes over these. Continue to draw and colour in the face as described throughout the previous chapter.

Sculpting a flat face

With the head drawn, you can begin to sculpt the face. To begin, always thread the needle with about a metre (yard) length of thread in a colour that matches the face colours as the stitching will 'disappear' – for clarity, I have used a black thread in the steps below. Secure the thread with a knot and two tiny 'anchor' stitches at back of the head, near the top.

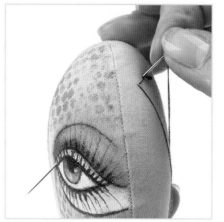

1 Bring the needle through from the back of the head to the right inner eye.

2 Take the needle back through the face slightly above the right inner eye dot, out at the left inner eye.

3 Take the needle back through the face slightly above the left inner eye dot, back to the right inner eye. Repeat steps 2 and 3 twice then pull the thread gently.

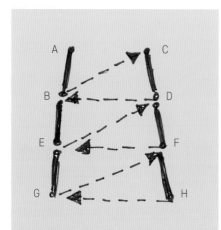

Order to stitch the nose

A down to B, then across and under the fabric, then out at C. Bring the needle down to D, then across and back out at B. Repeat this process all the way down the bridge of the nose.

4 Using the diagram, left, to help you, bring the needle through the fabric out at the top left-hand side of the bridge of the nose (A). Begin to stitch down each side of the nose, working in a zigzag pattern. Pull each stitch gently as you go, to raise and shape the nose and make it more three-dimensional.

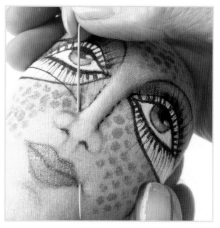

5 When you've reached the end of the bridge of the nose (G), bring the needle out at the right-hand corner of the mouth,

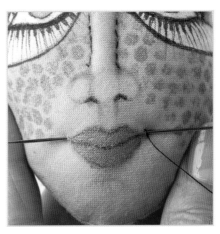

6 Take the needle through the fabric slightly above the stitch made at the right-hand corner of the mouth, out at the outer eye on the right-hand side of the face.

7 Take the needle back through the fabric, slightly above the outer corner of the right eye, and bring the needle back out at the right-hand corner of the mouth. Repeat steps 6 and 7 once more, pulling the thread gently at each stitch to create the cheek.

8 Take the needle through the fabric out at the left-hand corner of the mouth.

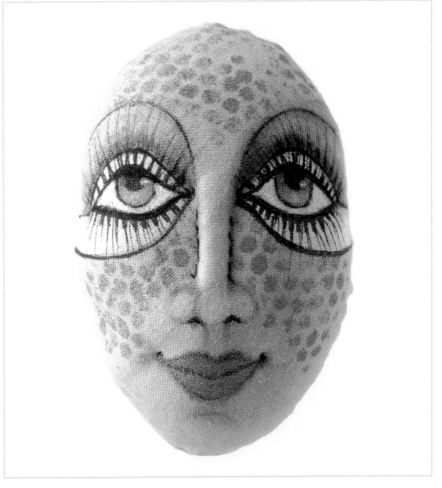

9 Take the needle through the fabric, slightly above the left-hand corner of the mouth and out at the outer eye on the left-hand side of the face. Follow the processes in steps 6 and 7 in a similar way, pulling the thread gently each time, to create the left cheek.

10 When the left side of the face is completed, take the needle through the outer corner of the left eye, right through the back of the head. Secure with two small anchor stitches, then cut the thread.

INSPIRATIONAL FLAT FACES

Yvette

I have always found the fashion and theatre designs by Erté, the Russian-born French artist, very inspirational. The cut and style of his clothes were quite revolutionary from the 1900s onwards: he used wonderfully rich fabric such as silk velvet and crepe de chine, which drape and flow beautifully around the body. I have used mostly antique fabrics for Yvette's costume, combining silver and black brocade, metallic lace, black silk velvet and silver beaded fringing.

The simplicity of Yvette's face is typical of Erté's models. He used simple lines to great effect, and the elegant, uncomplicated drawn features perfectly offset the flamboyancy and glitz of Yvette's turban headdress.

Jasmin

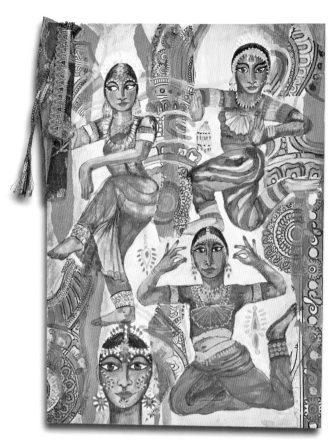

During the course of writing this book, I wanted to look at a whole range of faces and cultures. The vibrant costumes and poses adopted by classical Indian dancers inspired me to develop a design and tribute in cloth – Jasmin.

I used a light tan cotton, but you could use another 'flesh' tone or even dye the fabric yourself. As with Yvette, I chose to use simple lines to develop Jasmin's face. I also researched traditional Indian make-up, and was particularly inspired by traditional Bengali brides, who apply decorative patterns onto their faces as well as bold make-up.

Jasmin provided me with the opportunity to use wonderful, bright and colourful fabrics and braids. I also raided for local charity or op shops / thrift stores for appropriate jewellery. The necklace and earrings came as a set which was easy to dismantle, that I then placed on different parts of the costume. I found a beautiful bracelet, and it was the perfect shape and size for Jasmin's waist. In contrast to actual jewellery, brass curtain rings proved to be the perfect size for creating her bangles!

Oberon

I have long been fascinated by the playful fairies from Shakespeare's *A Midsummer Night's Dream*, and decided to create a cloth figure of one of the characters – Oberon, King of the Fairies. I always saw him as a bit of a grumpy character, but he was also very mischievous!

Although my Oberon has a flat face, I have drawn it in a more realistic style compared to Yvette and Jasmin, with shades, lines and contours to suggest expression and age.

Oberon's costume was influenced by the Shakespearean period, comprising of a doublet (a snug-fitting jacket for men) and hose (one or two garments for the lower body). However, I wanted the clothing to further suggest that Oberon was a woodland fairy, so for his cloak, collar and hat, I machine embroidered leaf-like designs onto water-soluble fabric.

MAKING A DIMENSIONAL HEAD

Unlike a flat face, which is made from only two pieces of fabric, a dimensional face needs four pieces of fabric to achieve a truly three-dimensional shape. The two front pattern pieces are particularly important as they will provide a realistic profile. Different-shaped profiles will enable you to create different characters. I have provided a basic head pattern and a few alternatives in the templates section, on pages 132 and 133.

For clarity, I have used a black thread in these steps. For your own doll, use a good-quality thread that matches the colour of your fabric.

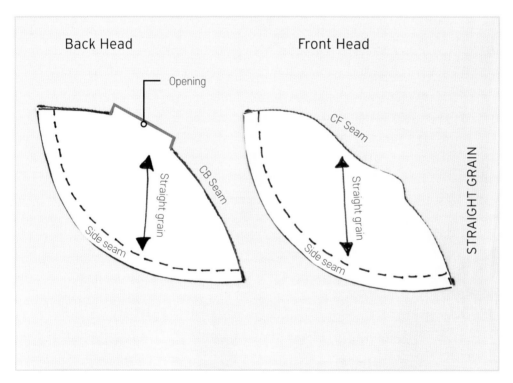

1 Iron the freezer paper pattern onto doubled fabric placed right sides together (see the freezer paper method on page 105), making sure the straight grain line is parallel with the straight grain of the fabric. Note there are two pieces of fabric being sewn together, layered over the top of each other.

With a small 1.5mm stitch set on your machine, sew down the centre front (CF) and centre back (CB) seams, leaving an opening (see the pink line) in the Back Head piece.

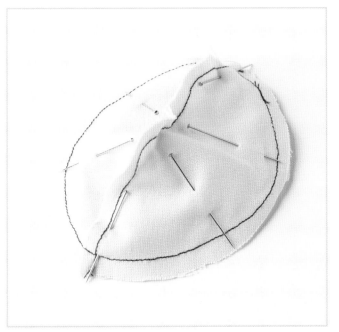

2 Cut out the head pieces: cut around the CF and CB seams first, adding a 4mm (just over ⅛in) seam allowance; then cut along both side seams, along the edges of the freezer paper – these side seams already have a seam allowance (see the dashed lines, opposite). Gently peel away the freezer paper (this can be used again for another doll). Open out both head pieces, then with the right sides facing, pin the Front Head and Back Head together. Make sure the chin and forehead seams match.

3 Starting at the top, sew all the way around the head. Once the whole perimeter of the head is stitched, trim the seams then turn the head right side out through the CB opening with forceps. Push out the seam of the head by inserting forceps through the opening and running it around the seam – this will give the head a good shape, ready for stuffing.

4 Stuff the head firmly, making sure you push the stuffing right into all the contours of the face. Fold the raw edges of the opening inside the head, then close the opening with temporary stitches, as in step 5 on page 58, or with pins to retain the stuffing while sculpting and drawing. Push a pin through one side of the nose and out the other; this will keep the stuffing in the nose while you needle sculpt.

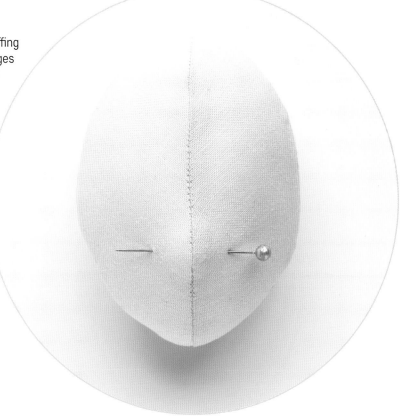

NEEDLE SCULPTING A DIMENSIONAL FACE

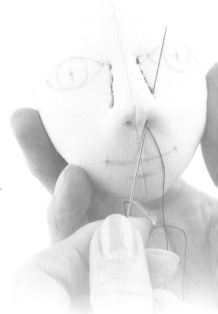

While the four-piece pattern of a dimensional head will help to create the three-dimensional form of the face, needle sculpting will enhance the features to create further realism, depth and character.

When needle sculpting, the stitches should be small so that, once the face is coloured, they will not show. Each stitch made should be pulled firmly to create the features; however, take care not to pull the thread too tightly or the features will become puckered and distorted. You may find some areas of the face will need to be stitched twice to ensure they hold their shape.

Use a fine strong thread and a long fine darning needle. For clarity, I have used a black thread in these steps. For your own doll, use a good quality thread that matches your fabric.

Marking out

Before sculpting, you will need to mark in the positions of the key features to ensure you needle sculpt correctly.

The lips and nose have already been established by the pattern's profile, but the other features will still need their positions marked.

Use a coloured pencil in a medium tone, such as ochre.

1 Begin by lightly marking the dividing lines on the head – use the guidance on Proportions of the Face on page 24 to help you.

2 EYE Draw the basic shape of the eyes, using the information in stages 1 and 2 on page 26 for guidance.

3 BRIDGE OF THE NOSE Draw a line either side of the centre-front (CF) seam. These lines should be narrower at the top, widening out at the bottom.

Tip

Don't draw the nose lines too close together at the top: when you are needle sculpting, you will be gently pulling the bridge of the nose together, and you could end up with a very thin nose.

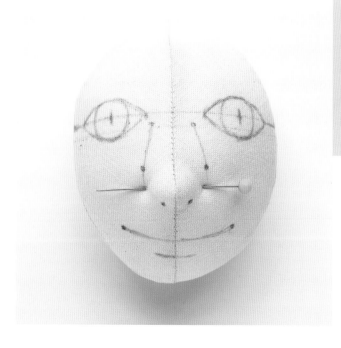

4 NOSTRILS Mark dots at the base of the nose, either side of the vertical line.

5 MOUTH Draw a line for the mouth about halfway between the nose and chin; draw a smaller line between the mouth line and chin to create the lower lip.

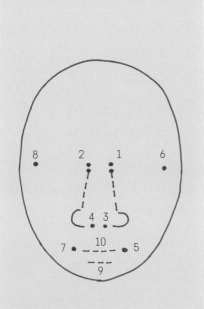

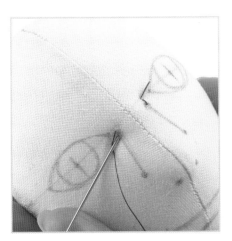

Main sections of a three-dimensional face to needle sculpt

1–4 = Nose

5–8 = Cheeks

9 and 10 = Mouth

Sculpting a dimensional face

To begin, always thread the needle with about a metre (yard) length of strong thread in a colour that matches your fabric – for clarity, I have used a black thread in the steps below. Secure the thread with a knot and two tiny 'anchor' stitches at back of the head, near the top.

STAGE 1: SCULPTING THE NOSE

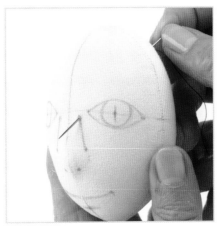

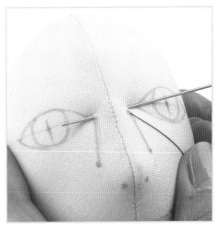

1 Bring the needle through from the back of the head to the top-right point of the nose (point 1 on the diagram, left).

2 Take a stitch in at the right inner dot (point 1), pass the needle through the nose and bring it out at the top-left point of the nose (point 2).

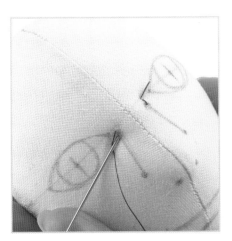

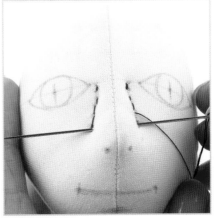

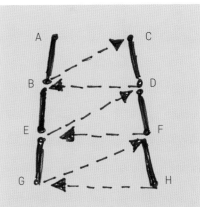

3 Repeat step 2 then pull the thread gently. Take a stitch back to point 1.

4 Using the diagram, right, to help you, bring the needle through the fabric at the top left-hand side of the bridge of the nose (A), and begin to stitch down the sides of the nose, working in a zigzag direction. Pull each stitch gently as you go, to raise and shape the nose and make it more three-dimensional.

Order to stitch the nose

A down to B, then across and under the fabric, then out at C. Bring the needle down to D, then across and back out at B. Repeat this process all the way down the bridge of the nose.

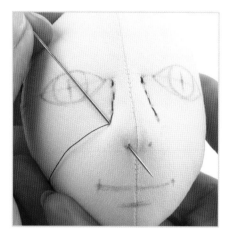

5 When you've reached the end of the bridge of the nose (point G), bring the needle out of the left nostril (point 4).

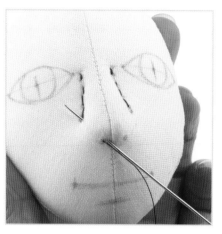

6 To create the nostrils, take a stitch up from point 4 to point G, then from G back to point 4. Finally, take a stitch through the fabric from point 4 to G. Pull the thread gently.

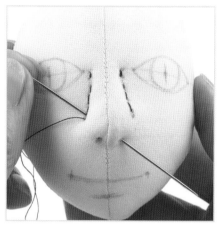

7 Take a stitch down to point 3.

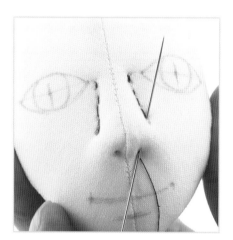

8 Repeat the process in step 6, taking the needle through the fabric several times between points 3 and H, to make the right nostril. Now you have the shape of the nose wings, you can draw them in.

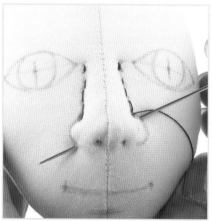

9 To begin forming the nose wings, take a stitch from the top right wing down to the bottom of the left nose wing.

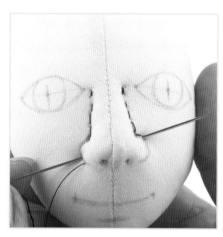

10 Take a stitch from the bottom of the left nose wing to the top of the right nose wing. Continue in this way, from the bottom to the top of the nose wing on one side, from the top to the bottom at the other to sculpt the nose.

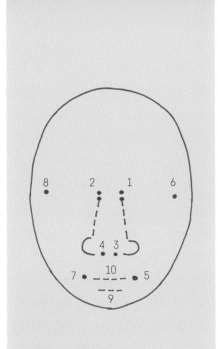

Main sections of a three-dimensional face to needle sculpt

1–4 = Nose

5–8 = Cheeks

9 and 10 = Mouth

STAGE 2:
SCULPTING THE CHEEKS

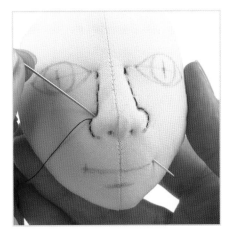

11 Finish sculpting the nose wing at point G then take a stitch down to point 5.

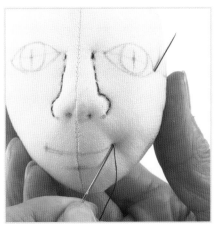

12 Take a stitch from the outer corner of the mouth (point 5) up to the outer eye (point 6).

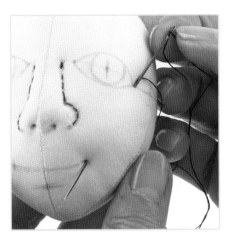

13 Take a stitch down from point 6 to the outer corner of the mouth (point 5).

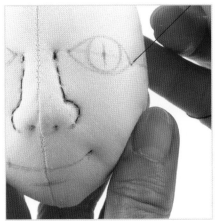

14 Take a stitch from point 5 back up to point 6 then pull the thread gently. Finally, take a stitch back down to point 5 – do not pull the thread this time.

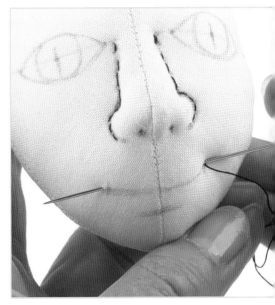

15 Take a big stitch under the fabric to point 7. Repeat the process in steps 12–14 at points 7 and 8.

STAGE 3:
SCULPTING THE MOUTH

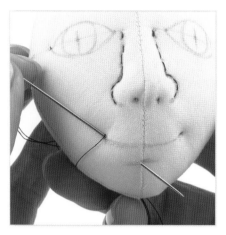

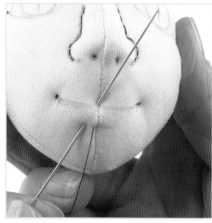

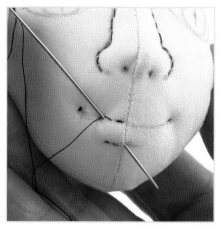

16 Bring the needle back to point 7 on the left-hand side of the mouth, then take a stitch from point 7 to the centre of the line for the lower lip (point 9).

17 Take a stitch from the lower lip to the middle of the mouth line (10).

18 Take a stitch back down to the lower lip line and then make another stitch back up to the mouth line. Finally, take a stitch down to the lower lip once again. You should have two stitches along the mouth line and two stitches on the lower lip line. Do not pull the thread too tightly at step 18, else you will end up with very thin lips.

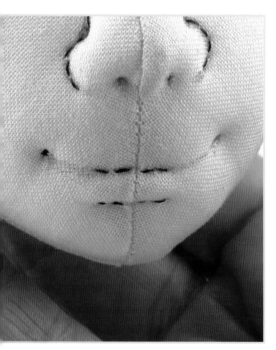

19 Repeat this process on the right-hand side of the mouth and lower lip.

20 To finish, take the needle through the right-hand corner of the mouth (point 5) and out at the outer right-hand corner of the eye (point 6). Take a stitch from point 6 through to the back of the head. Secure with two small anchor stitches before cutting the thread.

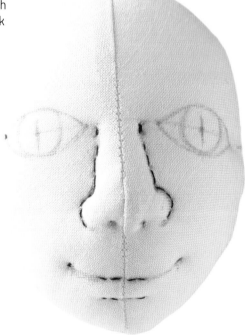

INSPIRATIONAL
DIMENSIONAL
FACES

Papillon

This creature was inspired by the beauty of butterflies, hence the name (*papillon* is French for 'butterfly'), with their delicate bodies, wonderful colours and intricate patterns.

The only trouble was deciding on the colour combination, as there are a vast number of butterfly species, and they come in so many amazing colours. After trawling through various source materials, I decided to create patterns from a selection of different butterflies, and use black, blue, purple and lime green as my main colours.

I wanted the face to resemble the colour and pattern of the wings, so instead of using coloured pencils I used acrylic paint to create the bold, solid patterns for Papillon's face.

Because the body is very plain, I introduced some texture by applying some heavy lace and scattered beading.

Carmen

This character doll is based on the 1940s Hollywood star Carmen Miranda, who was known for her carnival-style costumes and headdresses, and her exuberant personality.

Carmen's makeup was very colourful, and there was plenty of it! I have reflected this in the doll's face design, giving her luscious red lips, lots of eye shadow and bright rouge cheeks. Carmen Miranda also had very long, thick eyelashes, so I added luxurious lashes to the doll's face to complete this Hollywood image.

As far as the costume goes, the bolder the better! Frills, pompoms, faux fruit and brightly patterned fabrics are the trademarks of this fun lady.

The Ugly Sister

As that glorious musical *South Pacific* taught us, there really is nothing like a dame!

Based on the characters one can see at the pantomime, the Ugly Sister lends herself to a dramatic design, with over-the-top makeup and a garish costume. There is plenty of source material for pantomime makeup.

The head of this doll has a much more exaggerated profile compared to other dimensional-faced dolls, and has a turned-up nose. Her face is also quite pale, which serves to accentuate her strong eye makeup and long eyelashes. Round, rouge cheeks, bright pouty lips and, of course, her beauty spots complete this blowsy lady.

The costume for the Ugly Sister was inspired by seventeenth-century panniers, or side hoops, which formed part of a woman's undergarments to extend the width of her skirts.

EXTRA FEATURES

To complete your doll's face, and add further character and realism, specially made ears and hair can be attached to the head. For some dolls, eyes can be made more three-dimensional by adding eyelids and even – depending on the doll – attaching eyelashes.

MAKING EARS

It is not always necessary to put ears on a doll, as they are usually hidden by hair or headdresses; however, for fairies, elves and fantasy figures they are a very important part of their character. These ears can either be wired, which means they can be posed, or they can just be lightly stuffed and stitched. For all ears, cut out the necessary ear shape using the freezer paper method (see page 105).

The example below is a typical shape I use for a fairy ear; 'regular' ears are made in the same way. I am also using a contrasting thread for some steps; ensure that your own thread matches the fabric for the ears. Templates for regular and fairy ears are on pages 140 and 141.

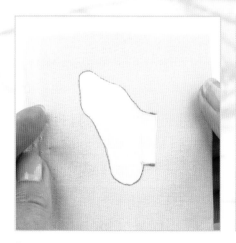

1 Iron the freezer paper pattern (I am using the male fairy ear on page 140) onto doubled fabric placed right sides together. Stitch around the ear template, leaving an opening as marked.

2 Cut out the ear with a 4mm (just over ⅛in) seam allowance all around, then turn through. Run forceps or a chopstick around the seam from the inside to push the ear into a nice shape. Lay a fine pipe cleaner/chenille stem on top of the ear and create an armature in the same shape as the ear, as shown. This gives the ear more form. With a flesh coloured pencil, draw in the inner ear shape.

3 Carefully place the pipe cleaner/chenille stem shape into the ear, through the opening.

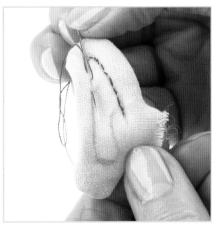

Tip
If you are not going to wire the ear with a pipe cleaner/chenille stem, leave out step 2, put a little bit of stuffing in, draw the inner line and machine or hand stitch along the line.

4 Once the armature of the ear is inside, fill the ear with stuffing. Don't add too much, insert just enough to pad it into a realistic shape.

5 Hand stitch over the draw inner ear outline. At this point make sure you have a right and a left ear!

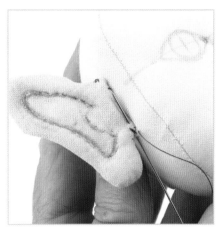

6 Once the inner ear is stitched, turn the raw edges of the ear opening inside and hand stitch it closed with whip stitch.

7 Align the top opening of the ear with the eye line on the side seam of the face and ladder stitch in place (see box below). First stitch on the back...

... then on the front. The placement of the ears can alter the character of the doll so try some variations. Experiment!

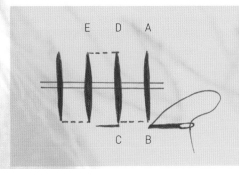

Ladder stitch

Ladder stitch is my preferred stitch for attaching facial features as it gives a flat finish and is almost invisible.

Bring the threaded and knotted needle up at A then down at B, on the opposite side of the opening. Take the needle through the fabric and across to C, then bring it back to the other side of the opening and down at D. Take the needle through the fabric and across to E. Continue in this way to seal the whole opening.

EYELIDS & EYELASHES

Eyelids can add another dimension of realism to dolls' eyes, and eyelashes a real touch of glamour. There are many fabulous eyelashes on the market – feather, glitter and even ones with rhinestones – so there is something to suit all tastes. I tend to add these details when creating dimensional faces. The template for this eyelid is on page 141.

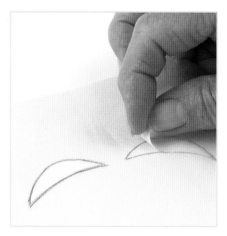

1 Cut out and attach the pattern pieces in using the freezer paper method (see page 105). Remember you will need a right and a left eyelid, so you will need to flip the eyelid before transferring the template. Iron the eyelids onto a single layer of fabric. Draw around the shapes with a coloured pencil.

2 Remove the freezer paper. Use a small brush to paint a little seam sealant over the pencil lines. Leave the eyelids to dry.

3 It is much easier to colour the eyelids before you cut them out. Use a soft pencil, acrylic paint or make-up to colour them in – you can choose neutral shades, or select more unusual colours for a glamorous effect.

4 With a pair of small sharp fabric scissors cut out the eyelids. Apply a fine line of glue to the lower edge of the eyelid. Stick the eyelashes along this edge and leave them to dry. Note there are longer eyelashes on one side – when you place the lid on the face, these should be closest to the side of the face, away from the centre of the head.

5 Apply a fine line of glue to the top edge of the eyelid.

6 Immediately lay the eyelid over the eye, on the 'socket', and pin in place. Use a toothpick or similar to gently press the top of the eyelid. Try to mirror the curve of the top of the eye and don't pull the eyelid flat – this will make the eyelid more three-dimensional and realistic.

ADDING HAIR

The hair should always be considered when designing a doll as it adds that extra bit of style and glamour. It is, quite literally, the crowning glory!

Below and overleaf are three methods that I use the most to create and add the hair to my dolls.

Needle felted hair

This is a creative and exciting technique to use for attaching hair to your dolls, and is quick and fun, too. The felting needle is a special, double-barbed needle; the barbs push the fibres into the stuffed head and secure them in place inside. Wool fibres, such as Wensleydale staples (or fleece), mohair, silk fibres and fancy wool yarns, are ideal for needle felting. It is not possible to needle felt synthetic hair; the method for attaching this is on page 87.

1 Arrange a small selection of snipped lengths of wool or other fibres for felting onto the head. Holding the needle vertically, gently but firmly stab the ends of the fibres into the head with the felting needle.

2 Continue to add fibres in small sections at a time to cover the crown of the head.

Extravagant hairstyles can be made by using wool tops, a continuous length of carded and processed wool. Simply wrap the length into your chosen shapes or style then gradually needle felt the hairstyle into place. I usually establish the style around the crown first, then any updos are secured afterwards.

WILD & SPIKY LOCKS

Wool yarn with a slub finish allows you to create a spiky effect with the fibres. Using colourful wool slub yarn has a wackier impact!

1 From the ball of wool slub yarn, cut small lengths at the narrowest point of the yarn.

2 Simply needle felt them onto the head, as shown on the previous page, stabbing them in at the fattest point of the length.

Wefted hair

This technique involves stitching (or 'wefting') together hair first, then attaching the joined lengths to the head to create long, lustrous locks.

   You can weft wool fibres or synthetic hair. If you wish to use wool fibres, I recommend selecting wool from any sheep or goat that has long staples or curls such as Wensleydale or Teeswater sheep, or a Mohair goat.

   Synthetic hair can be bought in many places, and it comes in a staggering variety of lengths, colours, curls and finishes. As the strands are already wefted together, you need only follow the stages below from step 3 to apply them.

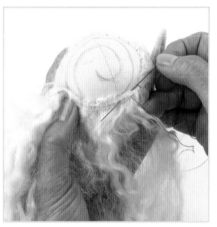

1 If you are using wool fibres, begin by teasing out the staples a little then lay the lengths together in a row. Lay a long length of strong fine thread over the staples, about 1.5cm (1in) down from the top. Carefully place your staples and thread under a sewing machine and zigzag stitch over the thread (set the zigzag stitch to a 1.5 width and a 1.5 length).

2 To secure the fibres together, fold the top edge over the zigzag stitching, then straight stitch underneath. Now wash the fibres (see below).

3 Stitch the top of the strip of wool fibres, or the top edge of the synthetic hair, to the head with whip stitch until the whole crown is covered. Stitch the hair to the head in a spiral direction, as shown, working from the outside inwards.

Washing wool fibres

Before moving on to step 3, you will need to wash the finished length of stitched wool fibres to remove all dirt and impurities, and felt the lengths together slightly.

1. Wash the stitched locks in warm water with a delicate washing detergent or conditioning shampoo two to three times.

2. Press the locks in a towel and leave to dry naturally.

3. When dry, gently comb the hair using a wide-toothed metal dog comb. Some stray ends may come out, but you should end up with a long continuous length of curly locks.

Tip
If you spray the dry locks with a water spray and leave them to dry, the fibres will spring back curly.

COLLAGE FACES

I wanted to explore the possibility of applying three-dimensional features to a flat face, but what started out as an experiment has developed into the production of some strange new beings! I have enjoyed the process of making these new characters, and I hope that you enjoy making them too.

The basic principles of making a collage face, and suggesting the personality of the doll in the way it is designed and constructed, are the same as for flat and three-dimensional faces: the shape of the face, the different features and the arrangement of those features will determine the character you want to achieve.

MAKING A COLLAGE HEAD

Collage heads are made in exactly the same way as flat heads (see page 58). The main differences are the types of fabric used, and the irregular shape of the head. As these dolls celebrate an abstract interpretation of a human face, I decided to experiment with different patterned and textured fabrics,

Here is just a selection of the head shapes one could use for a collage doll. I have provided templates for these on page 134. There is room for a great deal of creativity with these dolls – the fabric colour and head shape can strongly suggest the character of your doll.

MAKING COLLAGE FEATURES

I sometimes like to call these 'applied features' as they are made separately and then sewn onto the head, rather than drawn on like the flat and dimensional faces.

Collage doll features are made using the freezer paper method (see page 105), and there are two ways of sewing them up. With the first method, a slit is made at the back of the feature, and then roughly stitched together at the end (this method is shown below).

With the second method, an opening is left in one side seam – similar to the back piece of a dimensional head (see page 68) which is then sewn up with ladder stitch at the very end (see the diagram on page 83, if you need to remind yourself of how to work ladder stitch).

Technique

These steps demonstrate Method 1, which I tend to use when the back of the feature isn't visible, such as for mouths, hair, and eyebrows. For Method 2 follow the same steps, except at step 2 do not cut a slit and at step 4 hand sew with ladder stitch, not whip stitch.

1 Lay the template onto a doubled piece of your chosen fabric placed right sides together and pin it in place. Using a small stitch, machine sew all the way around the pattern piece.

2 Remove the template and cut out the feature, adding a 4mm (just over ⅛in) seam allowance all around. Transfer the opening marking from the template onto one side. Cut a slit along this line, in one layer of fabric only.

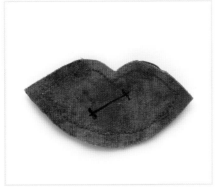

3 Turn the feature through the right way out, and push out all the edges with forceps or a chopstick.

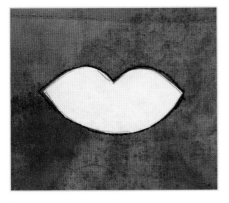

4 Stuff with a small amount of stuffing and stitch closed with whip stitches.

5 Once the piece is finished you can add some detail with topstitching.

Examples of sewn applied features

Please note these are not to scale. All of these features are made following either Method 1 or Method 2. For templates, see pages 135–137.

HAIR

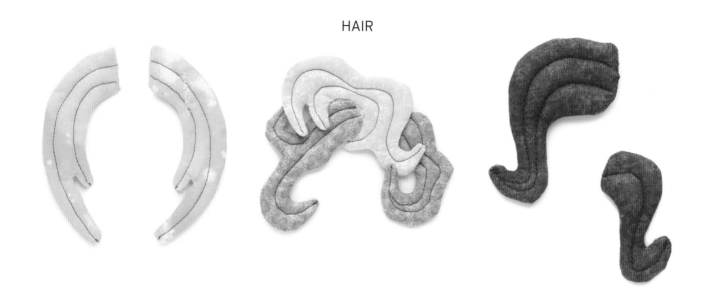

BEARDS & MOUSTACHES   EARS   EYELIDS

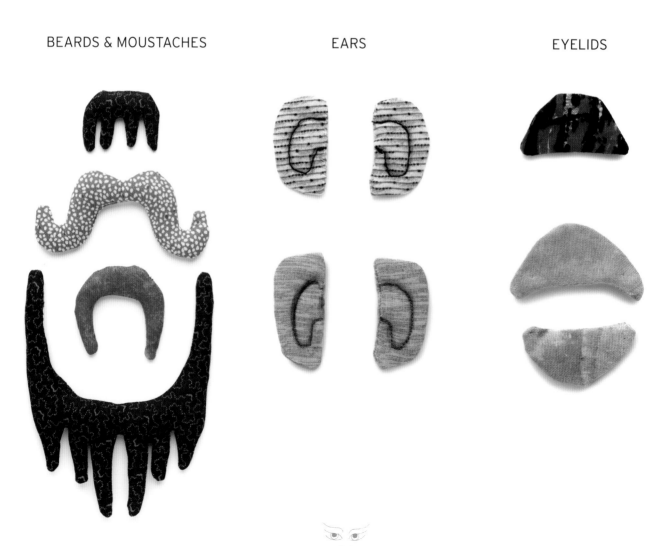

MOUTHS

NOSES

Making eyes

There are several methods that you can use to make eyeballs – from simple stuffed fabric eyes, or fabric-covered buttons or beads, to drawing eyes onto the fabric to add even more expression. The technique you choose will help build the character in your doll's face.

METHOD 1:
STUFFED FABRIC EYES

1 Using the eyeball template on page 135, cut a circle out of a single layer of your chosen eye fabric.

2 Run a gathering stitch around the outside of the circle, using a strong sewing thread.

3 Pull the tail of thread to draw in the edges of the fabric a little. Once a small cup shape is formed, put a little ball of stuffing inside (I have used forceps to help with this, as the eye is quite small!). Once stuffed, pull the thread tightly to close the opening, then secure with a couple of tiny whip stitches.

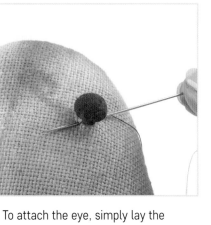

3 To attach the eye, simply lay the eye onto the head and work tiny whip stitches all around the eye, taking the needle through both the eye and head fabrics.

Choosing your fabric

The choice of fabric for your stuffed eyes will have an impact on the character of your doll. For this wise man, I used a black fabric patterned with flecks of gold, suggesting a magical, powerful figure.

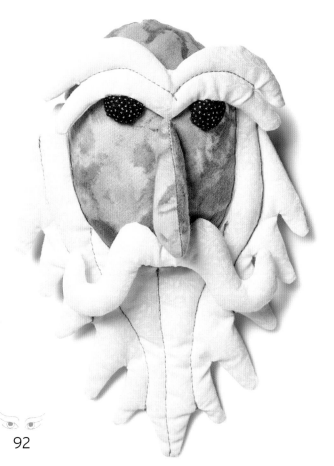

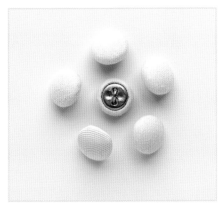

METHOD 2:
FABRIC-COVERED BUTTONS OR BEAD EYES

Like the stuffed fabric eyes, buttons and beads are a nice simple way to create eyes for your doll. They're also easy to attach. Simply choose your button or bead then sew it to the head through the button shaft or the hole in the bead.

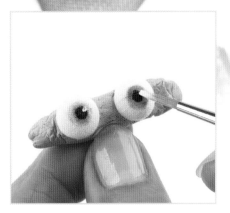

METHOD 3:
DRAWN-ON BUTTONS OR FABRIC

I've found that a small fabric-covered button works a treat as a surface for more detailed eyes, although stuffed fabric could be used, too. You will need colouring pencils, white acrylic paint and a black waterproof/fade-proof pen.

1 Press the button stalks into a piece of adhesive putty such as Blu-Tack®. This will hold the buttons securely temporarily, making them easier to colour in. Draw and colour in the irises with your chosen coloured pencil.

2 Draw in the pupils with the black waterproof/fade-proof pen.

3 Finish off the eyes by painting a white dot over each pupil, slightly off centre, to create a glint.

EXAMPLES OF EYES

Once you feel more comfortable creating a standard eye, you can add further details – why not try adding an eye highlight to a stuffed fabric eye, or draw the irises and pupils on a different part of the eye shape to create a different expression?

Here, I have attached eyelids over the eyes, to show how I tend to position them.

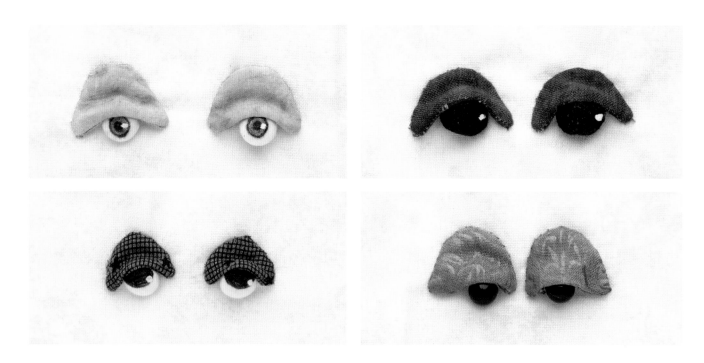

Attaching features

When all your features are ready, pin them into your desired positions on the head. Then, in turn, sew them in place all around with ladder stitch.

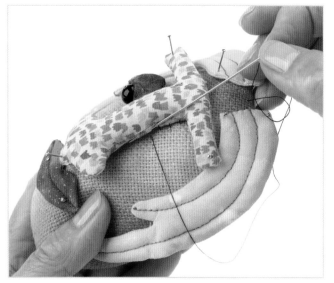

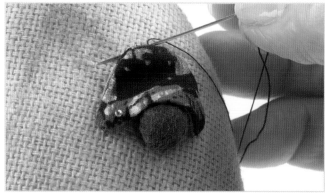

When attaching the eyelids, ensure your eyes are stitched on first to help with placement. Then, sew only around the top and side edges of the upper eyelids; for the lower eyelids, sew only around the bottom and sides.

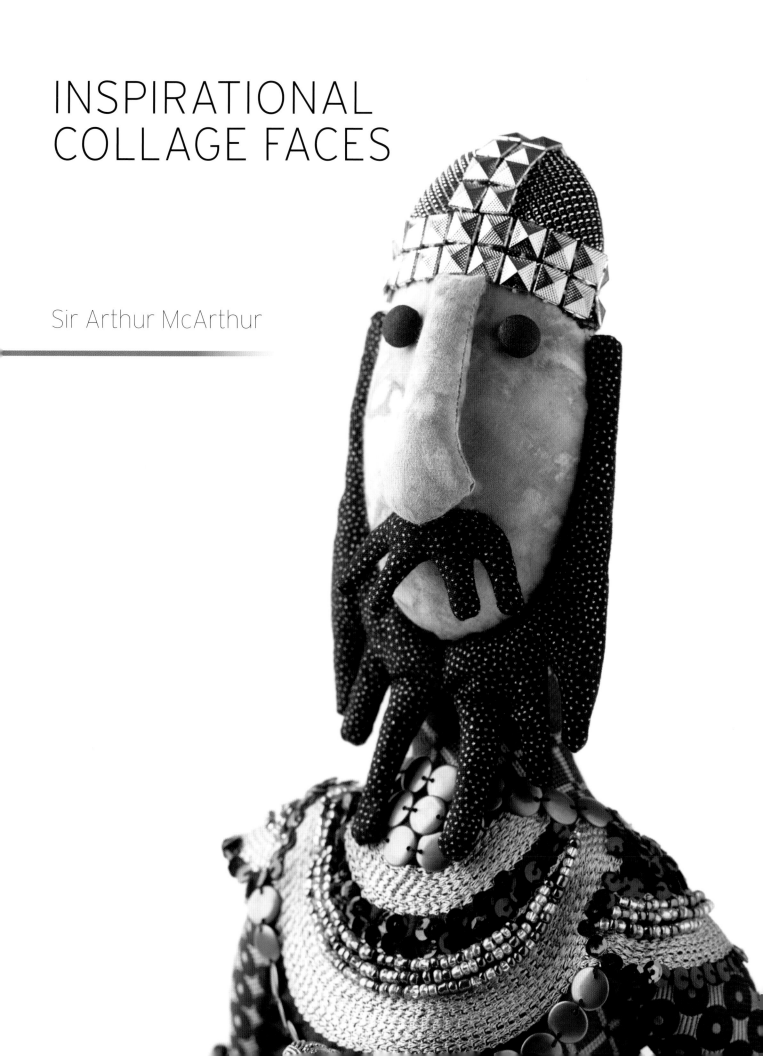

INSPIRATIONAL
COLLAGE FACES

Sir Arthur McArthur

If you ever go into a medieval church, take some time to look at the effigies lying peacefully on top of their tombs. I used their serene and simple features as my inspiration for this knight's face. I deliberately chose a pale blue, marble-effect batik fabric for the body and head, which further conveys this doll's solemnity and stillness. I was also inspired by a photo I took of a stone carving in a pillar or wall of a French church, depicting three saints (see the centre-bottom photo on page 18). I thought that the stylized lines of their flowing hair and beards were perfect for translating into abstract fabric shapes.

I also wanted to emulate the colours and textures of medieval armour. After trawling through my stash of fabric, I found patterned fabric and metallic trims which I thought evoked the essence of a medieval knight's costume – from faceted square spike beads and antique brass disc chains to black and gold ricrac and silver-plated buttons for the elbow joint.

Kissy Kissy

These two individuals evolved when I was experimenting with different-shaped heads and features. I finally chose a square head for one figure, made from a dyed, coarse linen; as a contrast, a delicate pale pink batik cotton was used to make the oval head for the other doll. As I added the facial features, the square-head doll became a man and the other a woman. This demonstrates how adaptive one can be with the doll design, even after creating a collage board as a reference. To accentuate the differences between the two dolls, I decided to add ears and short hair to the man's head, and have the lady's face with longer, wavy hair. The breasts for the lady have been deliberately designed to have an abstract appearance, and a template for them can be found on page 143.

Once I had the faces, I need to consider the body, limbs and clothes of these everyday characters. I wanted these figures to sit, so I chose to use a simple stump doll body with a flat base. The limbs are also simple tubular shapes, but are button jointed to allow for some movement. I used a pin-striped fabric for the man's arms and legs to suggest a business suit, and to add a little colour I made him a bold tie – this also works nicely with the bright pink of his lips. Although I used four different patterned fabrics for the lady's dress, the colours all work together effectively to create a dramatic yet coordinating outfit.

Wodaabe Dancer

When the men from the Wodaabe tribe in Niger perform at the Guérewol festival – an annual ceremony cum pageant where men court the Wodaabe women – they paint their faces and dress themselves in their finest clothes. They spend hours on their appearance, putting on brightly coloured fabrics, braiding their hair, decorating their clothes, hair and headdresses with beads, sequins and tassels – anything they can find is used to beautify their outfits to impress and catch the eye of the women.

I have used a dark brown batik fabric for the head and body, and added gold, orange and dark red features. These coloured and patterned fabrics add a richness to the face, complemented by the striking head wrap. In homage to the incredible adornments that the Wodaabe men wear, I have added a whole host of beads, tassels and trims to the already bold outfit of my doll, so that he is ready for his *Yaake* – the ritual dance.

Basic doll-making techniques

This section is devoted to the techniques I find most useful for doll making. It is always good to try new methods but at the end of the day, use the one you are most comfortable with.

Throughout the demonstrations I will be using a darker contrasting thread so that you will see where I am stitching. When sewing your doll, however, you should always use a good-quality thread to match your chosen fabric.

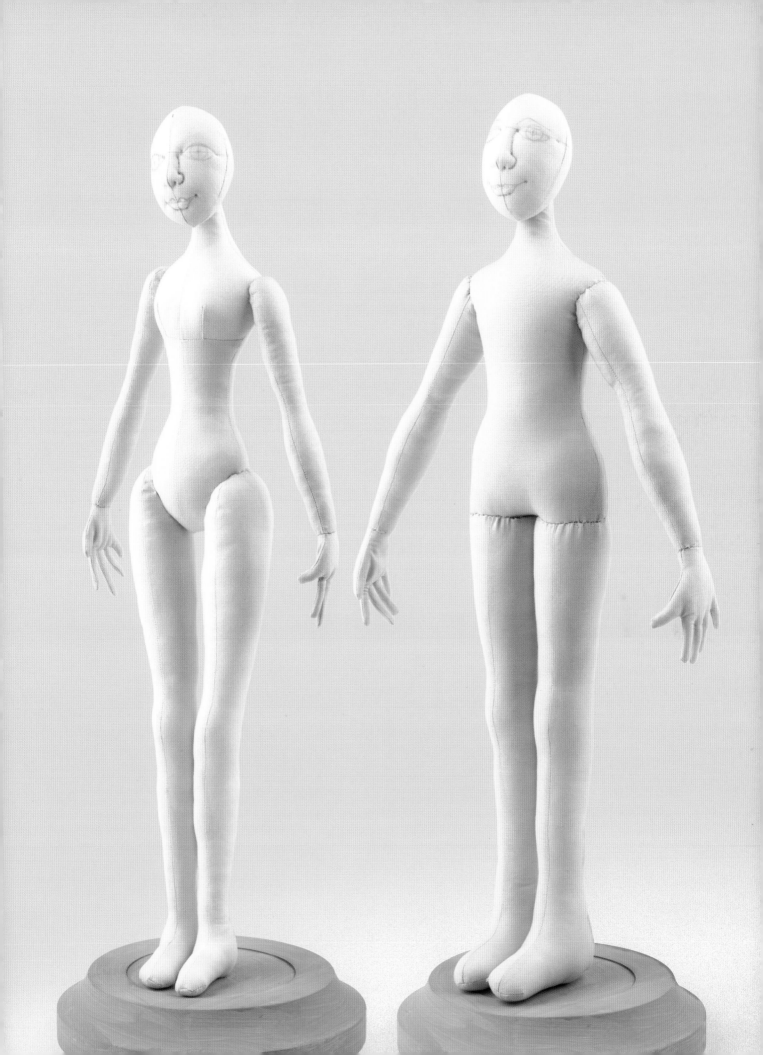

BEFORE YOU BEGIN

Sewing 101

Although many of the points below will likely be familiar to the experienced sewer, they are sufficiently important to bear being repeated when creating the bodies for your dolls.

- Always spend some time **familiarizing yourself with the pattern** before cutting out anything.
- To create a good strong seam that will withstand the strain of stuffing, **use a small stitch on your sewing machine** – this will be approximately 1.5mm in length.
- Use a **clear or open foot on your sewing machine**. This will enable you to follow the stitching line more easily.
- All seam allowances are 6mm (¼in), and about **4mm (just over an ⅛in) when trimmed**. If your allowance is too wide after trimming, it will create a lumpy finish; if it is too narrow, it will split under the pressure of stuffing.
- If the pattern has rounded or sharply concave areas, **clipping into the seams** (taking care not to snip into the stitching) will create ease in the fabric, and allow it to form intricate shapes. Common areas for this are the neck, elbows and knees.
- **Always cut off the ends of your threads**, as these can get trapped between the fabric and the stuffing and cause unsightly 'veins'.
- The **straight grain line on the pattern template** should be **parallel** with the straight grain of the fabric (and the **selvedge/selvage** – the uncut edge of the fabric).
- If the pattern requires two templates that correspond with each other, such as two leg pieces, ensure that the **matching notches** on one template correspond with those on the other.
- To enhance the shape, some patterns will include **darts**. To create the dart, cut into the triangle shape of the dart. Place the longer edges of the triangle together, the right sides of the fabric facing, and pin. Then, sew from the edge of the fabric to the narrowest point of the dart.
- **Openings** are indicated in one of two ways, depending on the type of pattern template. A gap may be marked partway along a sewn edge, or there may be protruding 'tabs' you cut around that are then folded inside the doll's body later.

Open foot (see also 'Sewing Kit' on page 12).

Key terms and symbols (refer to these when using the templates on pages 132-144)

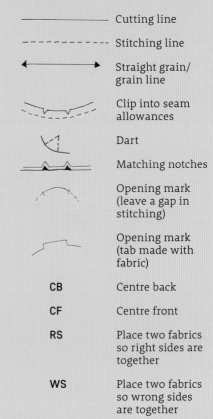

————————	Cutting line
- - - - - - - -	Stitching line
←——————→	Straight grain/ grain line
	Clip into seam allowances
	Dart
	Matching notches
	Opening mark (leave a gap in stitching)
	Opening mark (tab made with fabric)
CB	Centre back
CF	Centre front
RS	Place two fabrics so right sides are together
WS	Place two fabrics so wrong sides are together

Ladder stitch

Ladder stitch is my preferred stitch for sewing together the different body part as it gives a flat finish and is almost invisible.

Bring the threaded and knotted needle up at A then down at B, on the opposite side of the opening. Take the needle through the fabric and across to C, then bring it back to the other side of the opening and down at D. Take the needle through the fabric and across at E. Continue in this way across the whole opening.

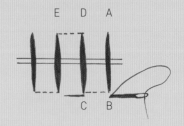

Transferring the pattern using freezer paper

As its name suggests, freezer paper is a domestic product but it is also used in the crafting world for template making – be it patchwork, quilting or doll making. It is a strong paper that is matt on one side and shiny on the other.

1 Place the freezer paper shiny side down onto the pattern diagram. With a propelling or sharp H pencil, trace off the pattern, marking any relevant information – straight grain, openings, matching notches, etc. Cut out the pattern.

2 Place the pattern pieces, shiny side down, onto the fabric and iron with a medium-hot iron. This will keep the pattern firmly in place while you are cutting out or stitching.

3 Use the edge of the freezer paper as a guide for stitching around the pattern or, if the seam allowance is included in the pattern, use the template to accurately cut out the required shape. Once the fabric is stitched or cut out, carefully peel the paper away. The pattern can be reused several times.

Joining patterns

Some of the larger pattern pieces, especially those for the legs, will need to be joined together. This is done before the fabric is cut out.

1 Lay the freezer paper shiny side down on to the top part of the pattern and trace. Make sure you mark in the notches.

2 Move the paper to the other part of the pattern; match the notch marks and trace to complete the whole pattern piece.

Stuffing

For the best results, always use a good-quality polyester toy stuffing. It needs to be soft and springy to the touch and not hard and dense. If you use the latter, it will go into balls and create 'cellulite'!

You will need a stuffing tool, such as a chopstick or a stuffing fork, for narrow or small doll parts. Forceps (or haemostats) are especially useful for stuffing.

Push a good handful of stuffing into your body part (small amounts tend to go into lumps) and gradually manoeuvre it into position with forceps or a stuffing fork, filling all contours and spaces before you move on to the next handful. Remember that you are stuffing a three-dimensional object, so you need to stuff from front to back then side to side.

A doll should be stuffed very firmly to achieve a good, smooth finish.

BASIC BODIES

Male dolls tend to have a straighter form than female dolls, with the legs attached to the base of the main body. Female dolls have wider hips, with the legs attached at the sides of the main body, and the front of the main body has several extra pieces for shaping the breasts. Otherwise, construction is virtually the same.

Pattern templates for both male and female dolls are on pages 138–142.

Male doll

BODY

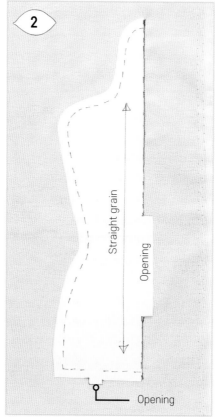

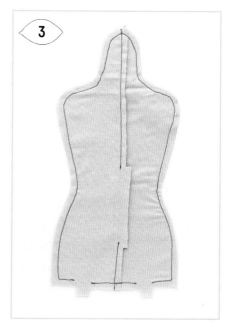

Straight grain

Opening

Opening

1 Iron the front body pattern template onto a single layer of your chosen fabric. Cut out the shape around the edge of the freezer paper.

2 Iron the back body pattern template onto doubled fabric placed right sides together and machine sew down the CB (centre back) seam, leaving the opening unstitched. Then, cut out along the CB seam, adding a 4mm (approx. ⅛in) seam allowance. Cut around the rest of the pattern along the edge of the paper. Carefully peel off the freezer paper.

3 With right sides facing, pin the back and front body pieces together then machine sew all the way around, leaving the openings unstitched.

4 Clip into the seam around the neck, then trim the rest of the seam. Turn the body right side out through the back opening.

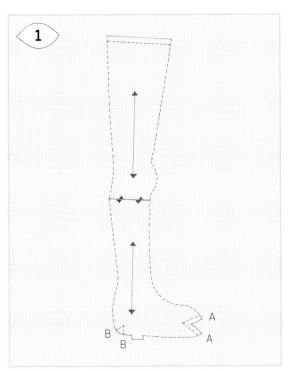

1

A
A
B
B

LEGS

1 Iron the joined leg pattern onto doubled fabric that has been placed right sides together. Machine sew all around the leg, leaving the top edge, the AA toe dart, the BB heel dart and the opening in the heel unstitched.

2 Trim the seams and cut into the darts.

3 Match the heel darts, bringing together B and B, then stitch along the dart. In a similar way, match the toe darts, bringing together A and A, then machine sew along the curved dart.

4 Turn the leg right side out through the opening at the top. Use forceps or a chopstick to press out the seams and give the leg a good shape.

5 Stuff the toe firmly, then insert a 61cm (24in) length of 4mm (approx. ⅛in) diameter armature wire through the heel opening and push it out at the top of the leg piece. Leave about 5cm (2in) of the armature hanging out below the heel. This will give you enough length to insert the doll into the stand, and hold the doll stable.

6 Gradually stuff the rest of the leg, adding a handful at a time and using forceps or a stuffing fork to push the stuffing gently but firmly right inside. Make sure you keep the armature wire in the middle of the stuffing.

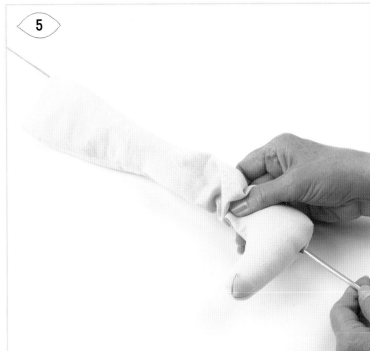

5

6

Tip

To avoid the dreaded 'cellulite' effect (see page 105), make sure the stuffing is pushed in well before you add any more.

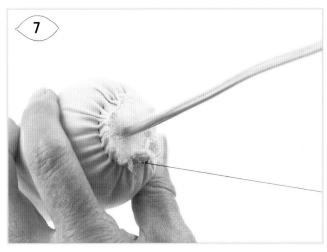

7 Run a gathering stitch around the top of the leg, then draw the thread to contain the stuffing. Repeats steps 1–8 to make up the other leg.

8 Feed each leg armature through the opening at the bottom of the body and out through the back opening.

9 Twist the armature wires together, as shown, or secure them together with thin wire. Use the pliers to help with this, if you wish.

10 Push the twisted wire back into the body and up into the neck section. Stuff the neck then the rest of the body firmly. Close the back opening with ladder stitch.

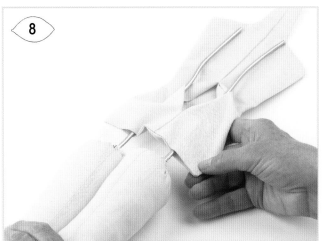

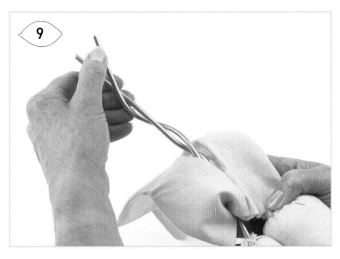

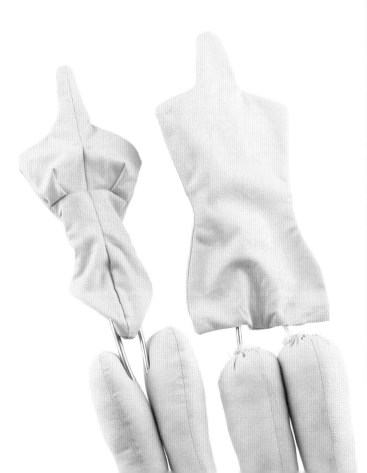

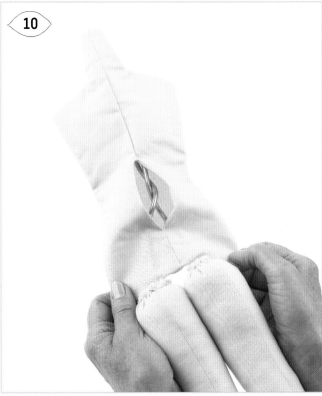

Female doll

BODY

1 For both the front and back body pieces, iron the pattern templates onto doubled fabric placed right sides together and machine sew down the CB (for the back pieces) and CF (for the front pieces), leaving openings unstitched.

2 Cut out all body pieces, adding a 4mm (approx. ⅛in) seam allowance to the CB and CF seams and cutting around the rest of the pattern along the edge of the paper. Carefully peel off the freezer paper.

3 Machine sew the darts right sides together in each upper front body piece.

4 Pin the bottom of the upper front body panel to the top of the lower front body panel (the under-bust seam). Machine sew right sides together.

5 Open out the front and back body pieces then pin them with the RS facing. Machine sew them together all the way around, leaving openings unstitched. Turn the body through the CB opening.

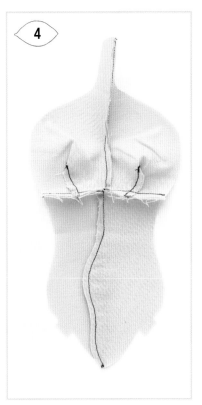

LEGS

1 The legs of the female doll are slightly different to the male doll's legs, as there are no heel darts; the tops of the legs are rounded, so that they will fit into the hips; and there are very small holes at the centre of the inner thighs where the armatures will exit.

Iron the leg patterns onto doubled fabric placed right sides together then stitch all around the leg, leaving the heel opening and toe dart unstitched. Trim the seams and cut into the dart.

2 Match the toe darts, bringing together A and A, then machine sew along the curved dart.

3 Mark the hole in the inner thigh for the armature (make sure you have a right and left leg). With a small pair of sharp scissors, make a very small cut in a single layer of the fabric. The armature needs to fit snugly within the hole, so it must not be too big.

4 Turn the leg through the opening at the back of the leg, and press all the seams with forceps or a chopstick to give the leg a good shape.

5 Stuff the toe then insert the armature as for the male doll (see page 107, step 5). Stuff the rest of the foot and leg, pushing in a little stuffing at a time with a stuffing fork or forceps. This method will help to prevent a lumpy finish. Make sure you keep the armature in the middle of the stuffing.

Both dolls

HANDS

As their name suggests, finger-turning tools are extremely helpful with this stage of the doll-making process. These consist of a metal tube and another thinner rod that can fit inside the tube.

1 Iron the freezer paper pattern onto doubled flesh-coloured fabric placed right sides together and stitch around the hand. Make sure you have two stitches between each finger and on the top of each finger. Repeat to make a second hand.

2 With a blunt cocktail stick dab a little seam sealant between each finger on both sides of the fabric. Leave the hands to dry.

3 Use a pair of small, sharp scissors to trim the seam and snip into the seams between the fingers. Because you have used the seam sealant to prevent the fabric from fraying, you will be able to cut right down to the stitching.

Tip

If you have folds at the base of your doll's fingers after you have turned them through, it means that you have not snipped into the seams enough between the fingers.

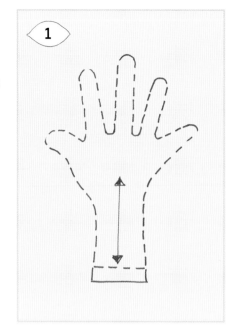

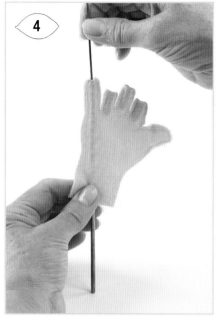

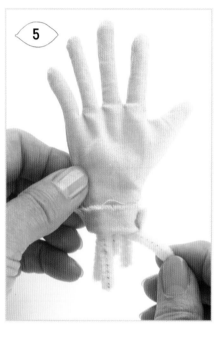

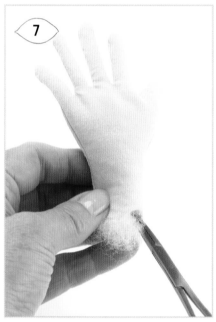

4 Turn each finger through by inserting the metal tube through the opening at the wrist, up into the finger. Place the thinner rod onto the tip of the finger. Hold the tube against a hard surface or against your body to keep it stable, then start to roll the finger up the rod a little at a time. Once all the tips of the fingers are turned through, turn the whole hand right side out via the wrist opening. Gently tug each finger to pull out completely.

5 For fingers, I use pipe cleaners/chenille stems as armatures as this enables more flexibility and movement. Try to select a size that fits snugly into your fingers; I tend to use 6mm and 9mm diameter pipe cleaners/chenille stems; if you can't find these sizes or another that is suitable, select a finer size then fold it over to make it thicker.

Measure each pipe cleaner/chenille stem from fingertip to wrist, adding an extra 1cm (⅜in) to the measurement – this allows you to turn one end over, preventing the end from piercing through

the tip of the finger. Snip the length required with sharp craft scissors. Once the ends are turned over, use forceps to insert the pipe cleaner/chenille stem into each digit.

6 Once all the digits are filled, twist the ends of the pipe cleaners/chenille stems together – wrapping one stem around the other four – to make a slim bundle for inserting into the wrist.

7 Add a little stuffing to the front and back of the hand to pad it out to a realistic shape.

ARMS

1 Iron the freezer paper pattern onto doubled flesh-coloured fabric placed right sides together then machine sew around the arm – if you are making the male arm, leave the top of the arm and the wrist section open; if you are making a female arm, sew around the curved top of the arm but leave an opening in the back seam. Repeat for the other arm, making sure you have a left and right arm.

2 Turn through and press under a small hem around the wrist of the arm.

3 Insert the wrist of one hand up into the bottom of the appropriate arm by approximately 2.5cm (1in) then pin it in place. Hand stitch all around the wrist to secure the hand, making sure you have a left and right hand.

4 Starting from the top of the arm, stuff down and around the pipe cleaner/ chenille stem bundle in the hand. Once the wrist section of the hand is completely stuffed, continue to stuff the rest of the arm, right up to the top. Note the photo below shows the male arm being stuffed; for the female arm, you will need to stuff the end of the hand and the arm through the opening in the side seam.

5 For the male arms, just like the leg (see page 108, step 7), work a gathering stitch around the top and pull the thread to contain the stuffing. For the female arm, close the opening in the back seam with ladder stitch.

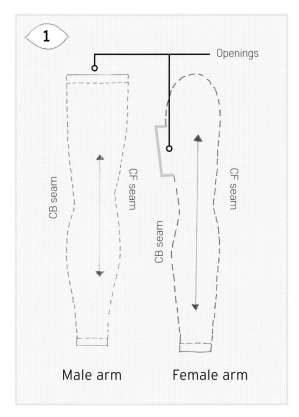

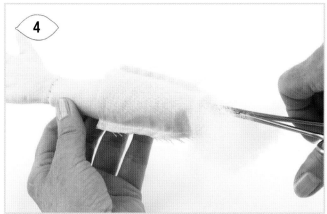

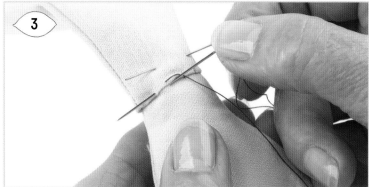

Openings

CB seam

CF seam

CB seam

CF seam

Male arm

Female arm

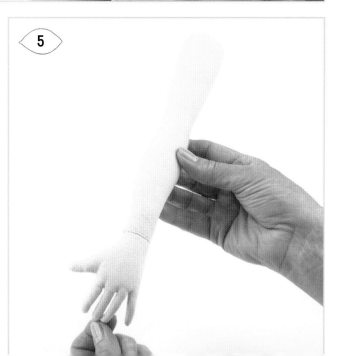

Male doll

SEWING THE LIMBS TO THE BODY

1 Pin the legs in place at the base of the body. Then, pin the appropriate arm to each side of the body – this may require a little bit of manipulation, to hide the gathered ends.

3 Secure the legs and arms to the body in turn with ladder stitch.

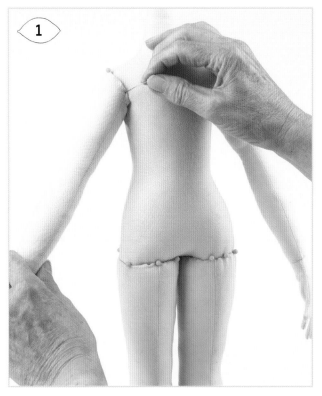

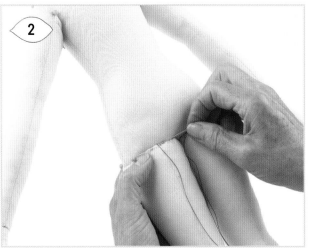

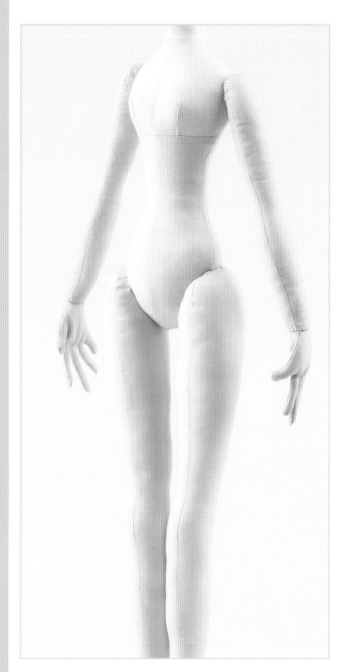

Female doll

SEWING THE LIMBS TO THE BODY

1 Pin the legs in place – remember that the female legs sit slightly at the sides of the body, rather than directly along the base of the body like the male.

2 Pin the appropriate arm to each side of the body.

3 Attach the legs and arms to the body with ladder stitch.

Both dolls

SEWING THE HEAD TO THE BODY

1 Remove the temporary stitches or pins from the back opening of the head. Turn in the raw edges of the opening, if necessary. With your thumb or a stuffing tool, make a little space in the stuffing.

2 Insert the neck into the space made and pin the head into position.

Tip

It is possible to pose the head to the side or up or down at this stage, and this can give your doll a bit more character.

3 Using strong matching thread, secure the head to the neck by hand sewing ladder stitches around the edge of the opening.

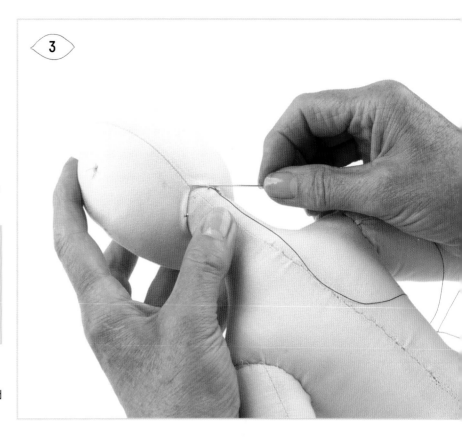

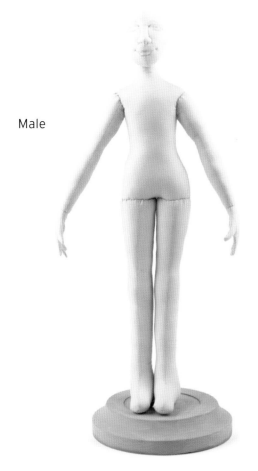

Male

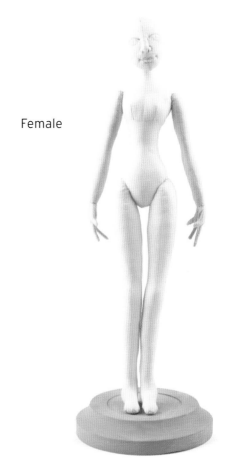

Female

BASIC COLLAGE BODY

The bodies of these dolls take the basic form of a 'stump doll' (a doll with no legs, able to 'stand' due to the flat base of the body). What makes them fun to make and work with is the unique way you can design, create and attach their limbs and three-dimensional features. Templates are on pages 143 and 144.

Body

1 Begin with the main body shape. Iron the freezer paper pattern (see page 143) onto doubled fabric placed right sides together (here, I've chosen a tie-dye effect batik fabric). Machine sew around the sides and top, leaving the base and the opening in the side seam unstitched. Cut out the sewn body with a 4mm (approx. ⅛in) seam allowance, then turn through the open base. Turn under a small hem and press.

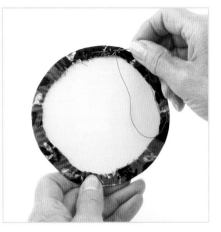

2 Cut out the body base pattern from card (see page 144), then use this to cut out a circle of fabric, adding a 6mm (¼in) seam allowance all around. Work gathering stitch all around the edge of the fabric. Place the card in the middle of the circle of fabric, facing the wrong side, and gently pull the thread to gather the fabric around the card.

3 Run some PVA glue around the edge of the fabric to make it secure. Leave this to dry completely.

4 Pin the main body shape to the card side of the base, matching the joining notches.

5 Sew the two together with overstitch, using a strong matching thread.

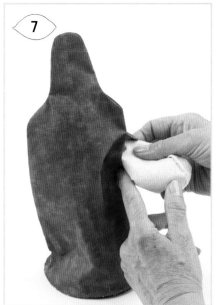

6 To help the doll 'stand' stably, weight bags are made and inserted into the base of the doll. I tend to use cheap calico fabric for this, and fill the bag with steel pellets. If you find these difficult to get hold of, poly granules, sand or dried lentils could be used, too.

Iron the freezer paper pattern (see page 144) onto doubled fabric and machine sew almost all the way around, leaving the opening unstitched. Cut out the fabric, then turn the bag through the opening.

7 Fill the bag with approximately 300g (10¾oz) of steel pellets or your chosen filling, then machine sew the opening closed. Push the weight bag through the opening in the body and position on the base.

8 Stuff the body firmly, then hand sew the opening closed with ladder stitch.

Breasts

1 Iron the paper pattern (see page 143) onto your chosen doubled fabric, placed right sides together. Machine sew almost all the way around, leaving the opening unstitched. Clip into the fabric at the central indent of the breasts.

2 Turn through the opening and stuff lightly. Hand sew the opening closed with ladder stitch.

3 Pin the breasts to the body, so that the opening is touching the body and the front projects out, then secure with ladder stitch.

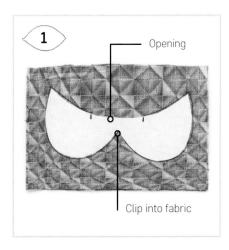

Opening

Clip into fabric

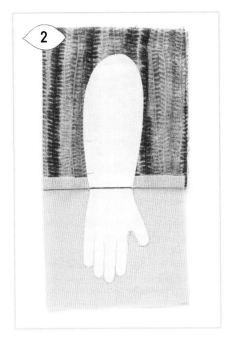

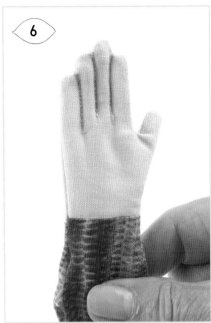

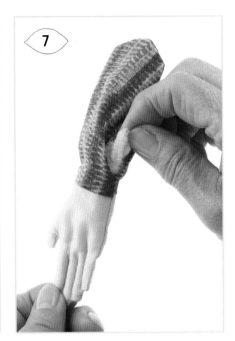

Hands & arms

FOREARM

1 Cut a strip of your chosen fabric for the hand (this could be flesh coloured or a more alternative fabric!) measuring 18 x 8cm (7 x 3in), and a strip of fabric for the arms or arm sleeves measuring 18 x 12cm (7 x 4¾in). Machine sew the two strips together on the longest side (18cm/7in edge).

2 Fold the fabric in half widthways, right sides facing, to double it. Place the freezer paper pattern (see page 143) on the fabric, laying the dividing line between the hand and arm along the seam joining the two fabric strips together – the hand should sit on the flesh-coloured fabric and the arm section on the patterned fabric. Iron in place.

3 Machine sew around the hand with flesh-coloured (or an appropriate coloured) thread, then switch to a matching thread to continuing sewing the arm.

4 Use the blunt end of a chopstick to dab a little fabric sealant in between the thumb and fingers and leave to dry.

5 Cut out the all-in-one forearm. Use a pair of small sharp scissors to snip into the fabric between the thumb and fingers. Turn through the forearm using finger-turning tools (see page 110).

6 Using the pattern template as a guide, mark in each finger with a soft colouring pencil, then hand or machine stitch down each finger line with flesh-coloured or matching thread.

7 Insert pipe cleaners/chenille stems into each digit. Once all are in place, twist one end around the other four to make a slim bundle. (See also steps 5 and 6 on page 110.)

8 Add a little stuffing to the front and back of the palms and then stuff the rest of the arm. Once the forearm is lightly stuffed, hand sew the opening closed with ladder stitch.

9 Repeat the steps to make the other forearm.

UPPER ARM

10 Iron the freezer paper pattern (see page 144) onto doubled fabric placed right sides together. Machine sew around the upper arm, leaving the opening unstitched.

11 Turn the arm through the opening and press. Stuff the arm lightly then close the opening with ladder stitches.

JOINING THE ARMS

12 Overlap the two arms – upper arm over forearm – then, with a long doll needle and strong thread, take several stitches through both limbs. The arms need to be mobile, so you should not make the stitches too tight. Place a button over the upper arm, over the stitches, then continue to stitch backwards and forwards through both limbs via the buttonholes.

13 For extra movement and security, make a 'shank' between the two arms by winding the thread around the stitches in between the limbs.

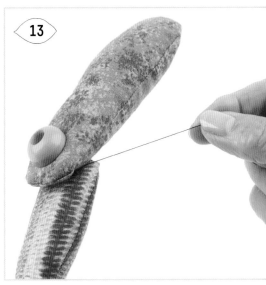

Legs

Legs are made in exactly the same way as the upper arms (see steps 10 and 11, opposite), and the upper and lower legs are joined together following the process above (see steps 12 and 13).

Head

To attach the head, follow the instructions for the realistic doll on page 113.

Templates

All templates are 100 per cent to scale, including the faces. The completed faces can be seen on the pages indicated.

SIMPLE LINE FACES (SEE PAGES 42 AND 43)

Simple long face #1

Simple long face #2

Simple long face #3

Simple long face #4

Simple long face #5

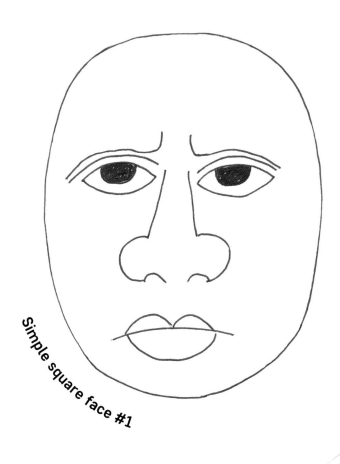

Simple square face #1

Simple square face #2

Simple square face #3

Simple square face #4

Simple square face #5

Simple oval face #1

Simple oval face #2

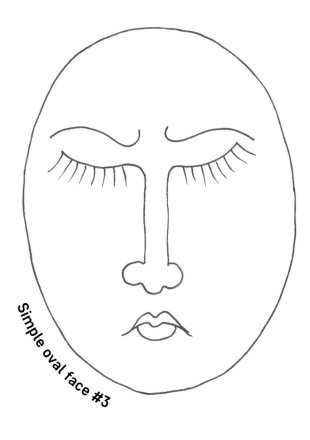

Simple oval face #3

Simple oval face #4

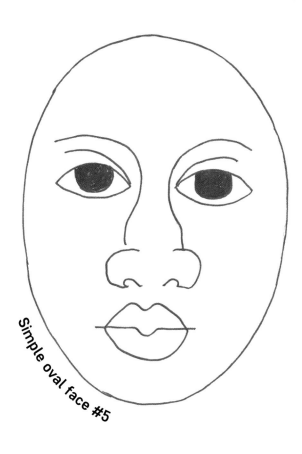

Simple oval face #5

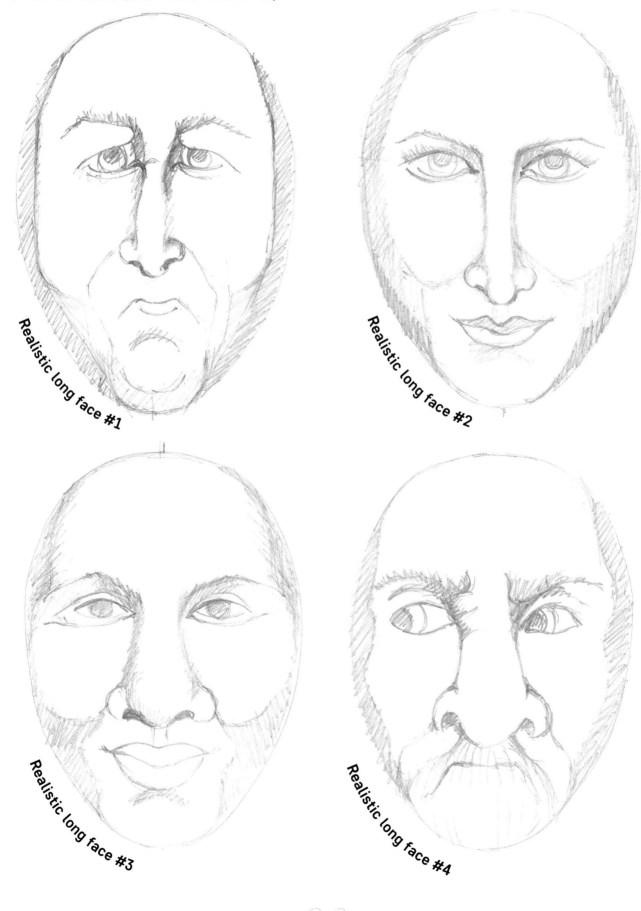

Realistic long face #1

Realistic long face #2

Realistic long face #3

Realistic long face #4

Realistic long face #5

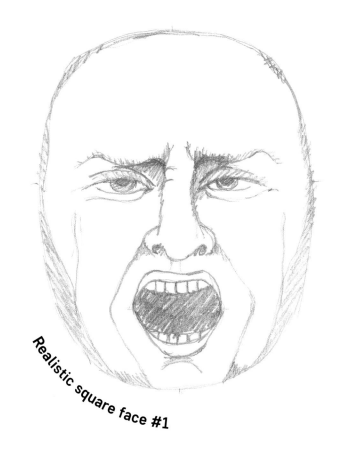

Realistic square face #1

Realistic square face #2

Realistic square face #3

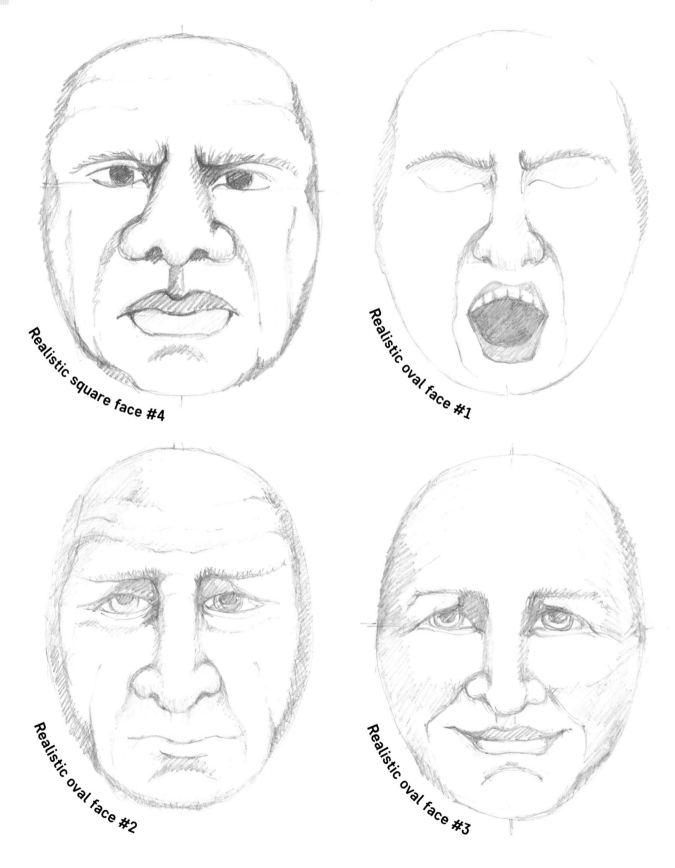

Realistic square face #4

Realistic oval face #1

Realistic oval face #2

Realistic oval face #3

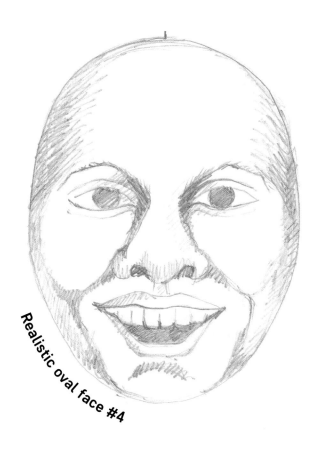

Realistic oval face #4

Realistic oval face #5

DECORATIVE FACES (SEE PAGE 50)

Decorative long face #1

Decorative long face #2

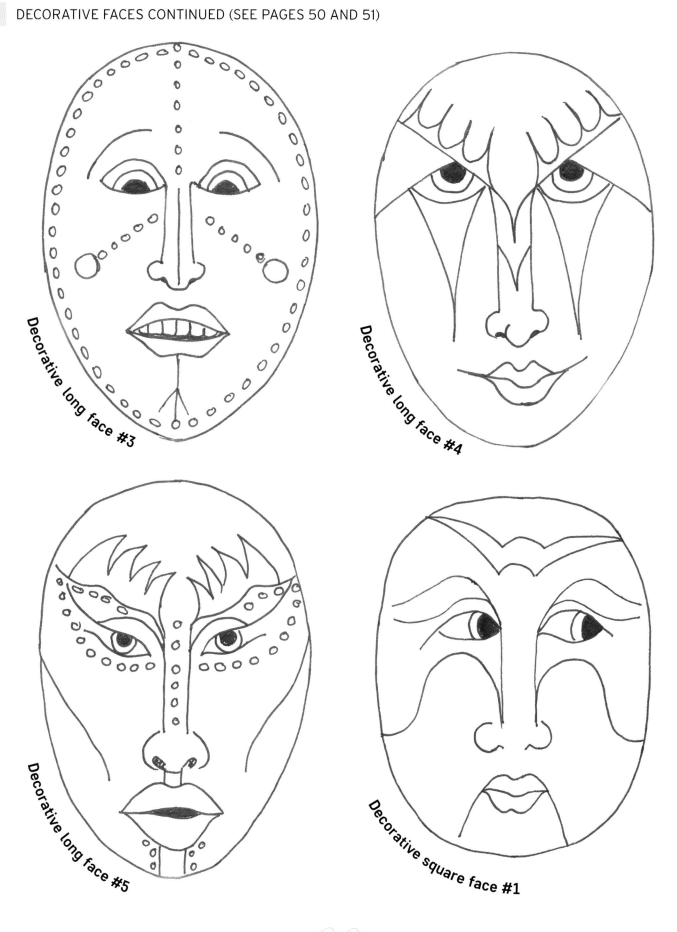

Decorative long face #3

Decorative long face #4

Decorative long face #5

Decorative square face #1

Decorative square face #2

Decorative square face #3

Decorative square face #4

Decorative square face #5

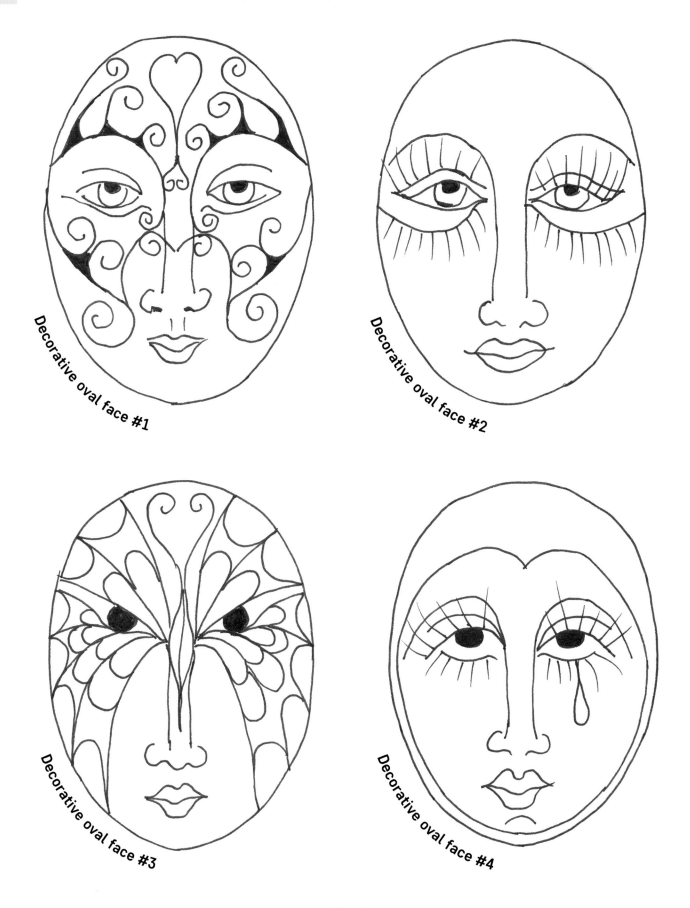

Decorative oval face #1

Decorative oval face #2

Decorative oval face #3

Decorative oval face #4

Decorative oval face #5

Collage face #1

Collage face #2

Collage face #3

COLLAGE FACES CONTINUED
(SEE PAGES 54 AND 55)

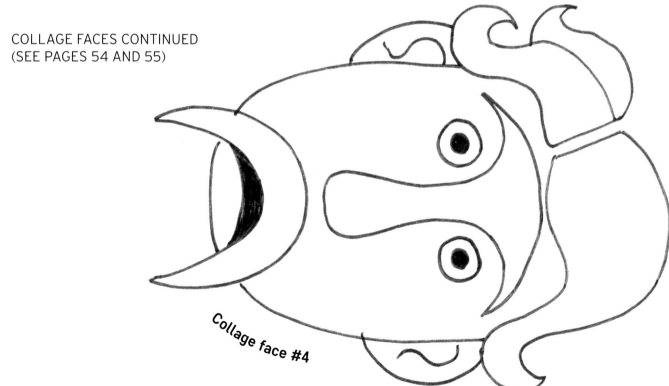

Collage face #4

Collage face #5

Collage face #6

FLAT FACES (SEE PAGE 58)

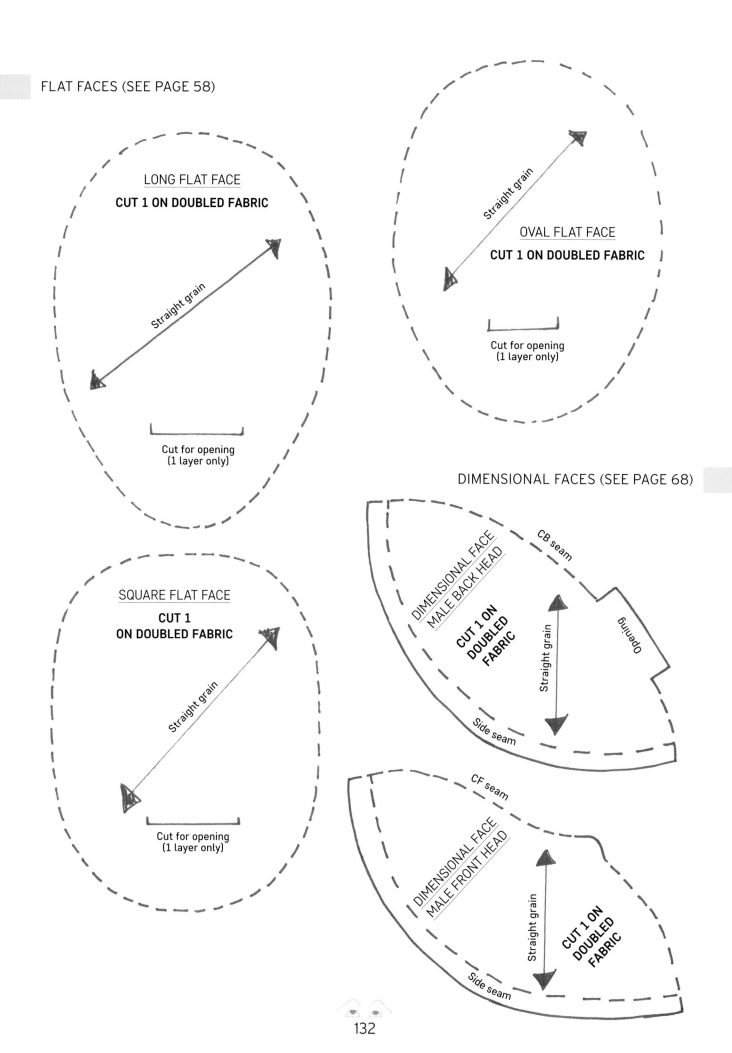

LONG FLAT FACE

CUT 1 ON DOUBLED FABRIC

Straight grain

Cut for opening
(1 layer only)

OVAL FLAT FACE

CUT 1 ON DOUBLED FABRIC

Straight grain

Cut for opening
(1 layer only)

SQUARE FLAT FACE

**CUT 1
ON DOUBLED FABRIC**

Straight grain

Cut for opening
(1 layer only)

DIMENSIONAL FACES (SEE PAGE 68)

DIMENSIONAL FACE
MALE BACK HEAD

**CUT 1 ON
DOUBLED
FABRIC**

CB seam

Opening

Straight grain

Side seam

DIMENSIONAL FACE
MALE FRONT HEAD

CF seam

**CUT 1 ON
DOUBLED
FABRIC**

Straight grain

Side seam

DIMENSIONAL FACES CONTINUED (SEE PAGE 68)

CB seam
FEMALE – BACK HEAD
Straight grain
Opening
CUT 1 ON DOUBLED FABRIC
Side seam

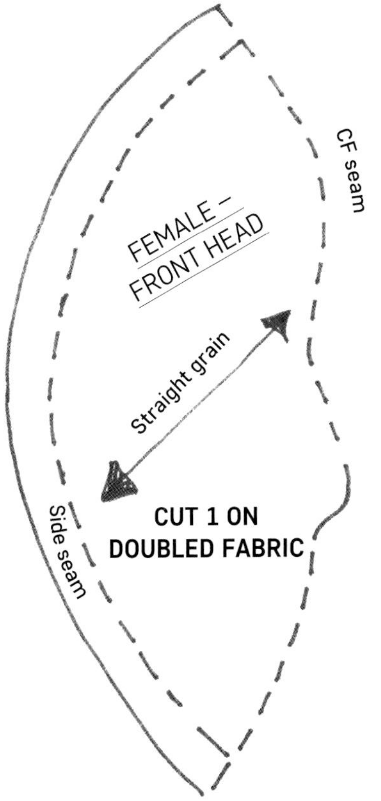

CF seam
FEMALE – FRONT HEAD
Straight grain
Side seam
CUT 1 ON DOUBLED FABRIC

CF seam
CHARACTER – FRONT HEAD
CUT 1 ON DOUBLED FABRIC
Side seam
Straight grain

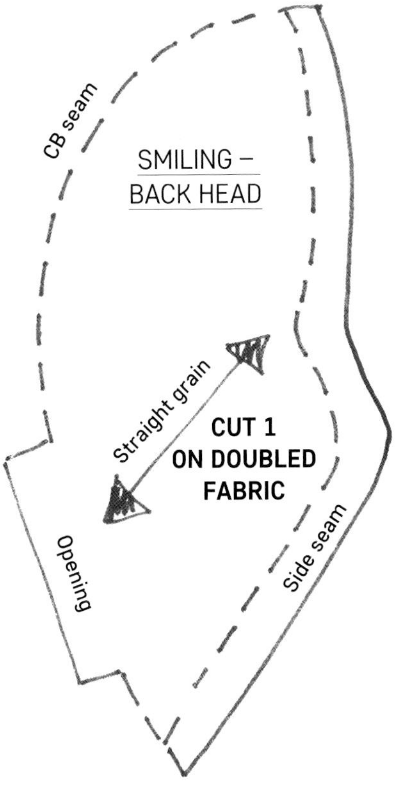

CB seam
SMILING – BACK HEAD
Straight grain
CUT 1 ON DOUBLED FABRIC
Opening
Side seam

CF seam
SMILING – FRONT HEAD
Straight grain
Side seam
CUT 1 ON DOUBLED FABRIC

CB seam
CHARACTER – BACK HEAD
Straight grain
Side seam
CUT 1 ON DOUBLED FABRIC
Opening

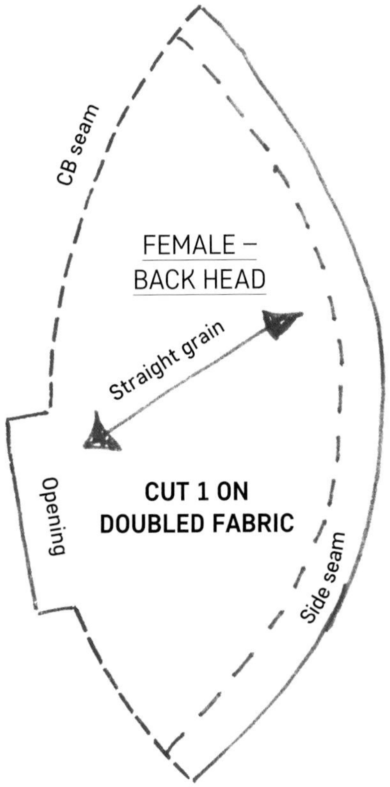

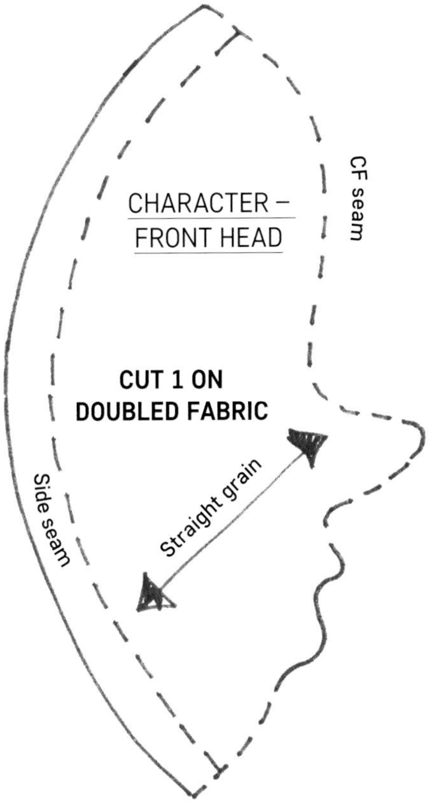

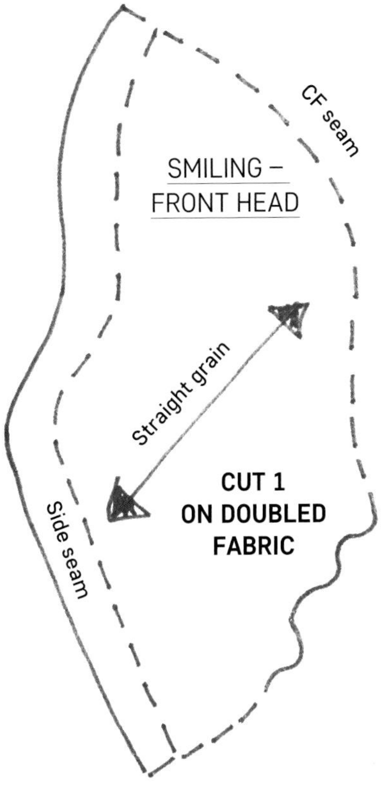

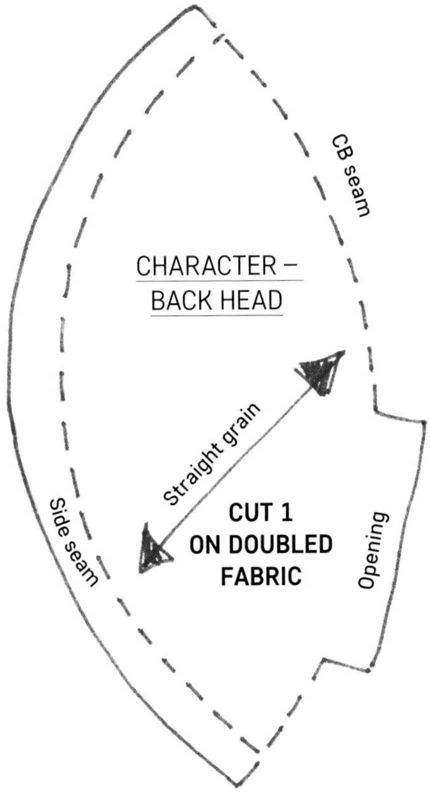

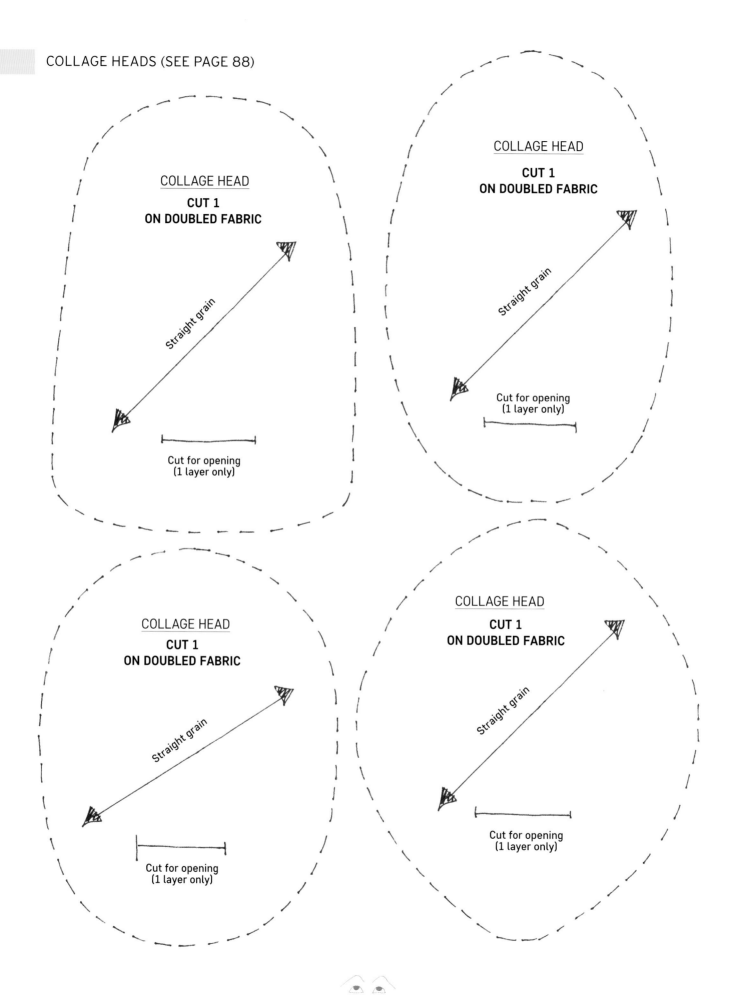

COLLAGE HEAD
**CUT 1
ON DOUBLED FABRIC**

Straight grain

Cut for opening
(1 layer only)

COLLAGE HEAD
**CUT 1
ON DOUBLED FABRIC**

Straight grain

Cut for opening
(1 layer only)

COLLAGE HEAD
**CUT 1
ON DOUBLED FABRIC**

Straight grain

Cut for opening
(1 layer only)

COLLAGE HEAD
**CUT 1
ON DOUBLED FABRIC**

Straight grain

Cut for opening
(1 layer only)

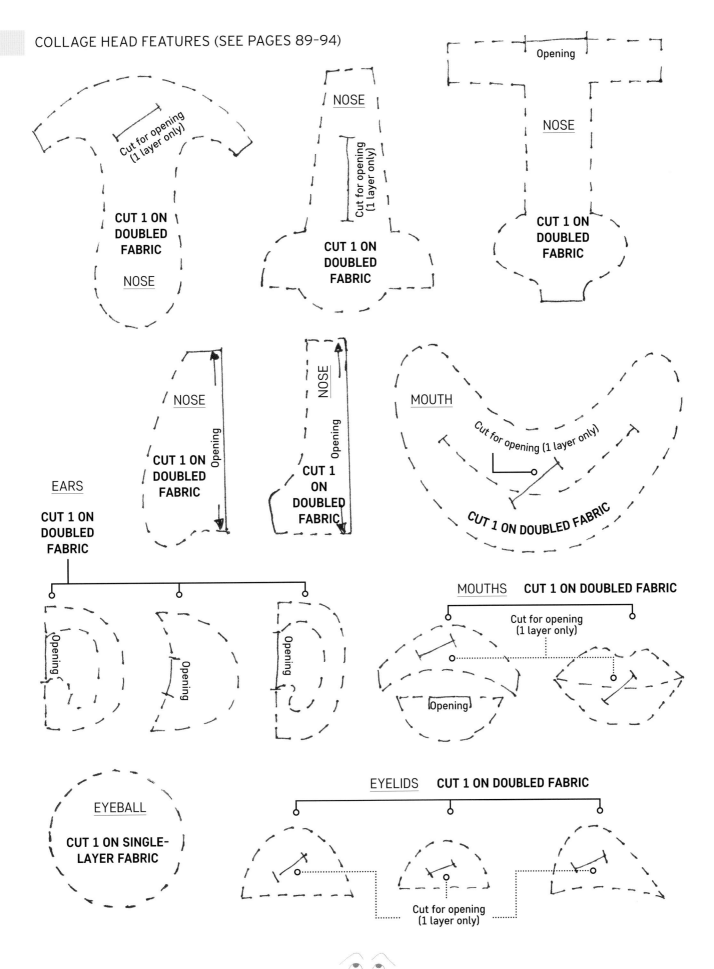

NOSE

Cut for opening
(1 layer only)

CUT 1 ON
DOUBLED
FABRIC

NOSE

NOSE

Cut for opening
(1 layer only)

CUT 1 ON
DOUBLED
FABRIC

Opening

NOSE

CUT 1 ON
DOUBLED
FABRIC

NOSE

Opening

CUT 1 ON
DOUBLED
FABRIC

NOSE

Opening

CUT 1
ON
DOUBLED
FABRIC

MOUTH

Cut for opening (1 layer only)

CUT 1 ON DOUBLED FABRIC

EARS

CUT 1 ON
DOUBLED
FABRIC

Opening

Opening

Opening

MOUTHS   CUT 1 ON DOUBLED FABRIC

Cut for opening
(1 layer only)

Opening

EYEBALL

CUT 1 ON SINGLE-
LAYER FABRIC

EYELIDS   CUT 1 ON DOUBLED FABRIC

Cut for opening
(1 layer only)

MOUSTACHES

CUT 1 ON DOUBLED FABRIC

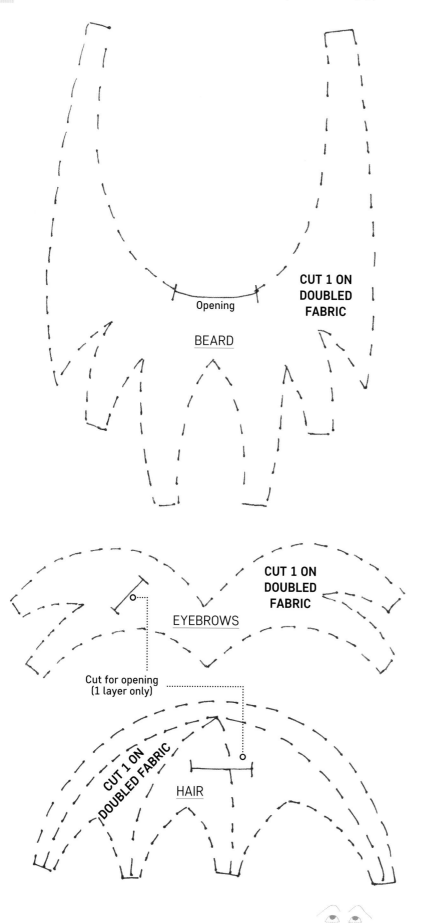

Opening

CUT 1 ON DOUBLED FABRIC

BEARD

CUT 1 ON DOUBLED FABRIC

EYEBROWS

Cut for opening
(1 layer only)

CUT 1 ON DOUBLED FABRIC

HAIR

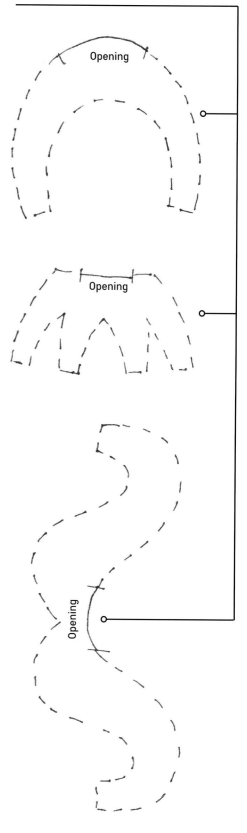

Opening

Opening

Opening

COLLAGE HEAD HAIR (SEE PAGE 90)
– FOR ALL, CUT 1 ON DOUBLED FABRIC

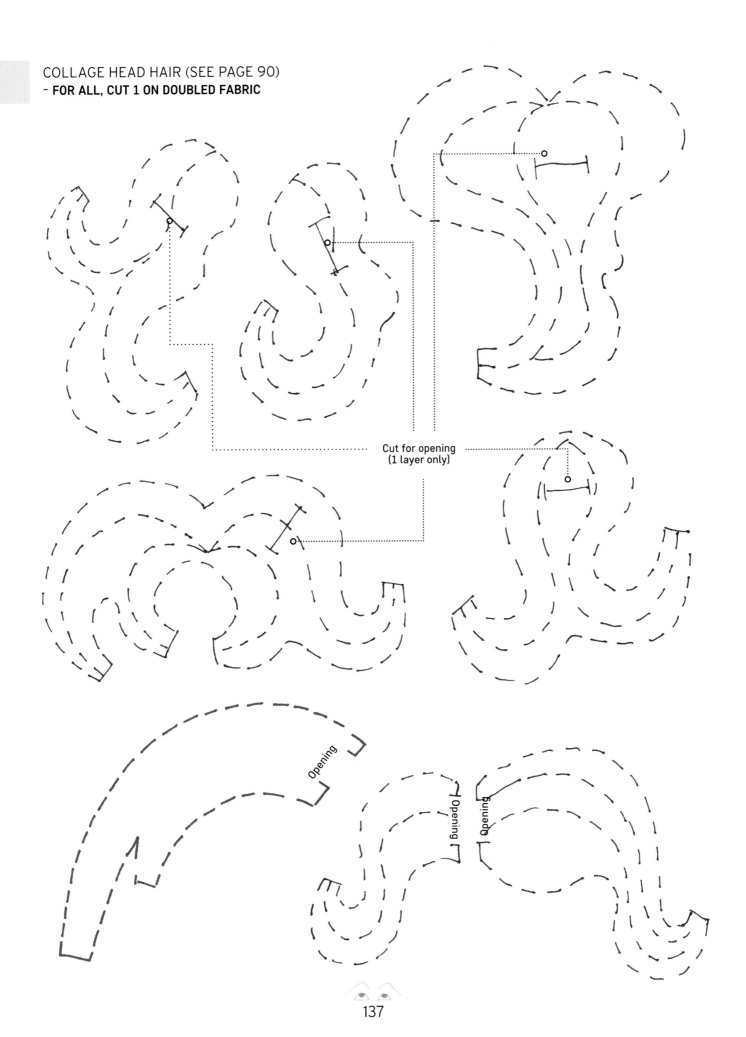

Cut for opening
(1 layer only)

Opening

Opening

Opening

BASIC MALE DOLL
(SEE PAGES 106-113)

Straight grain
MALE – FRONT BODY
CUT 1 ON SINGLE-LAYER FABRIC
MALE – HAND
CUT 2 ON DOUBLED FABRIC
Straight grain
Opening
Opening
Opening

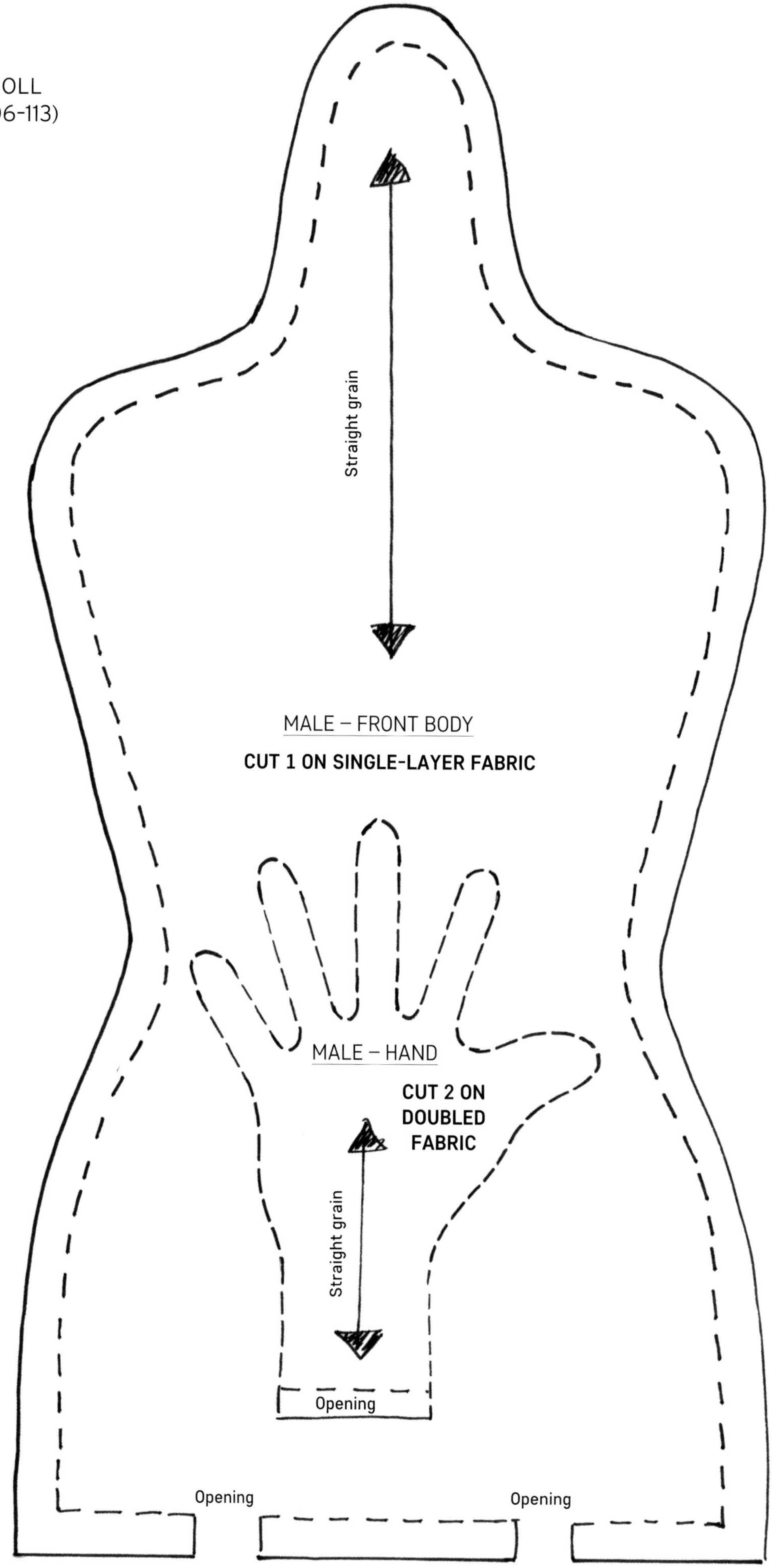

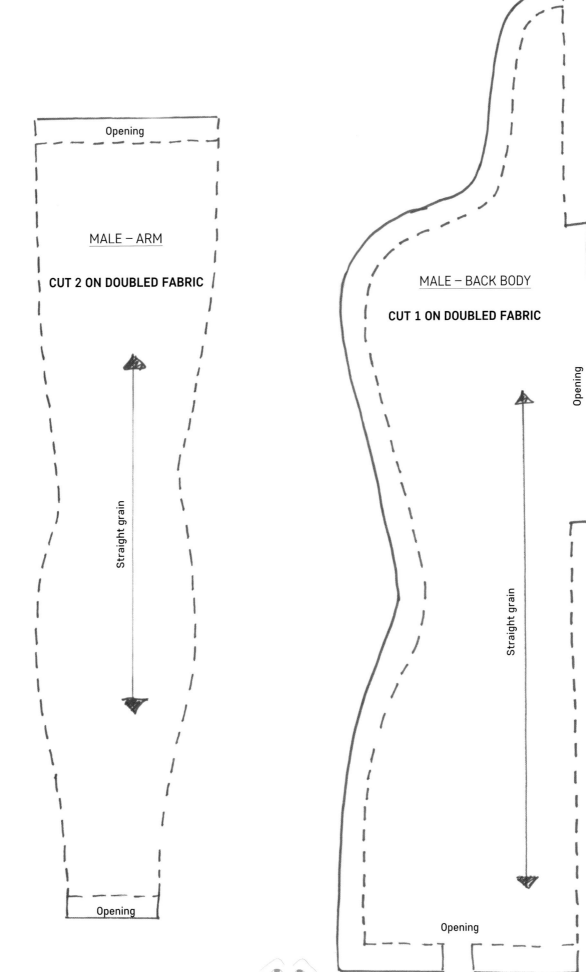

MALE – ARM

CUT 2 ON DOUBLED FABRIC

Opening

Straight grain

Opening

MALE – BACK BODY

CUT 1 ON DOUBLED FABRIC

Opening

Straight grain

Opening

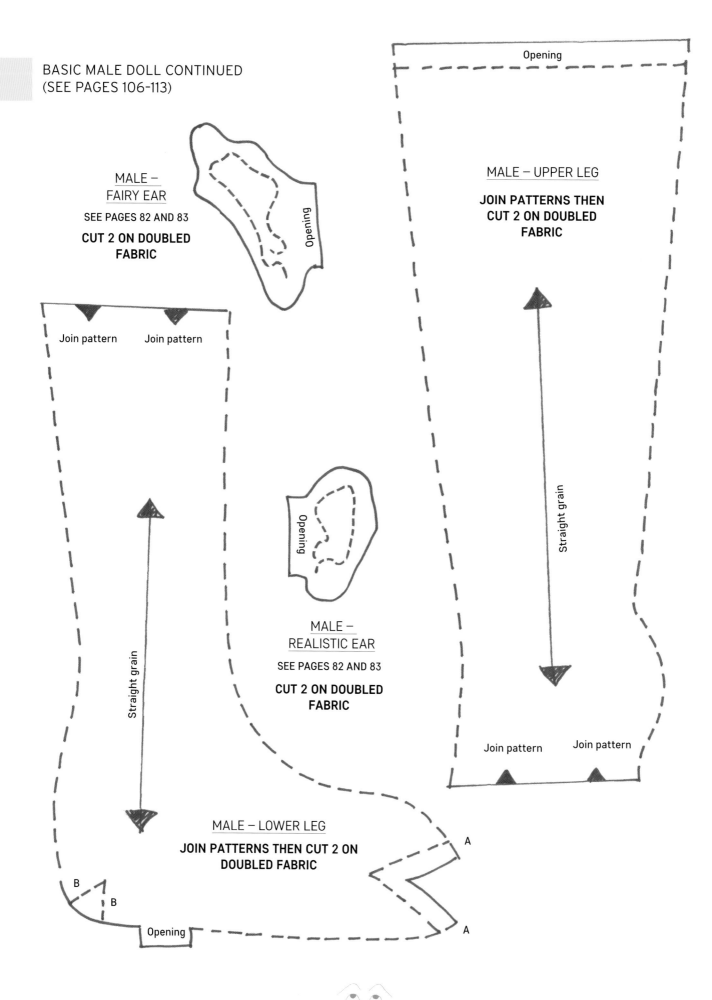

MALE –
FAIRY EAR

SEE PAGES 82 AND 83

CUT 2 ON DOUBLED FABRIC

Opening

MALE – UPPER LEG

JOIN PATTERNS THEN CUT 2 ON DOUBLED FABRIC

Straight grain

Join pattern   Join pattern

Join pattern   Join pattern

Straight grain

Opening

MALE –
REALISTIC EAR

SEE PAGES 82 AND 83

CUT 2 ON DOUBLED FABRIC

MALE – LOWER LEG

JOIN PATTERNS THEN CUT 2 ON DOUBLED FABRIC

Straight grain

A

A

B

B

Opening

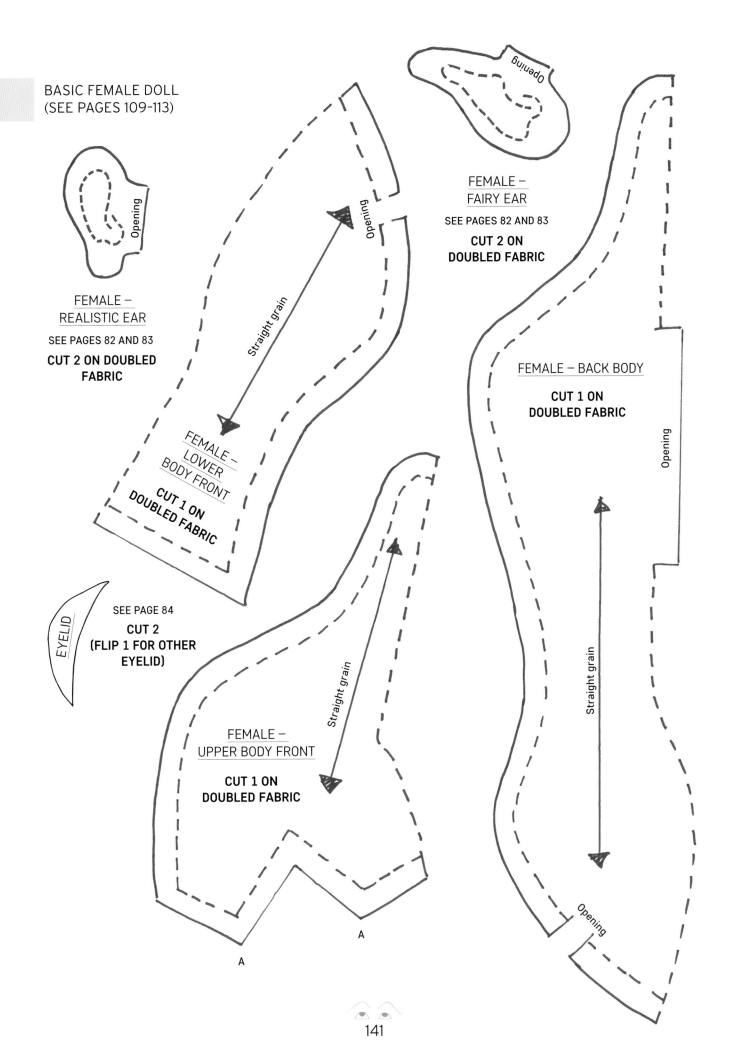

BASIC FEMALE DOLL
(SEE PAGES 109-113)

FEMALE –
REALISTIC EAR

SEE PAGES 82 AND 83

CUT 2 ON DOUBLED FABRIC

FEMALE –
FAIRY EAR

SEE PAGES 82 AND 83

CUT 2 ON DOUBLED FABRIC

Opening

Straight grain

FEMALE –
LOWER
BODY FRONT

CUT 1 ON DOUBLED FABRIC

FEMALE – BACK BODY

CUT 1 ON DOUBLED FABRIC

Opening

EYELID

SEE PAGE 84

CUT 2 (FLIP 1 FOR OTHER EYELID)

Straight grain

FEMALE –
UPPER BODY FRONT

CUT 1 ON DOUBLED FABRIC

Straight grain

Opening

A

A

REALISTIC FEMALE DOLL
(SEE PAGES 109-113)

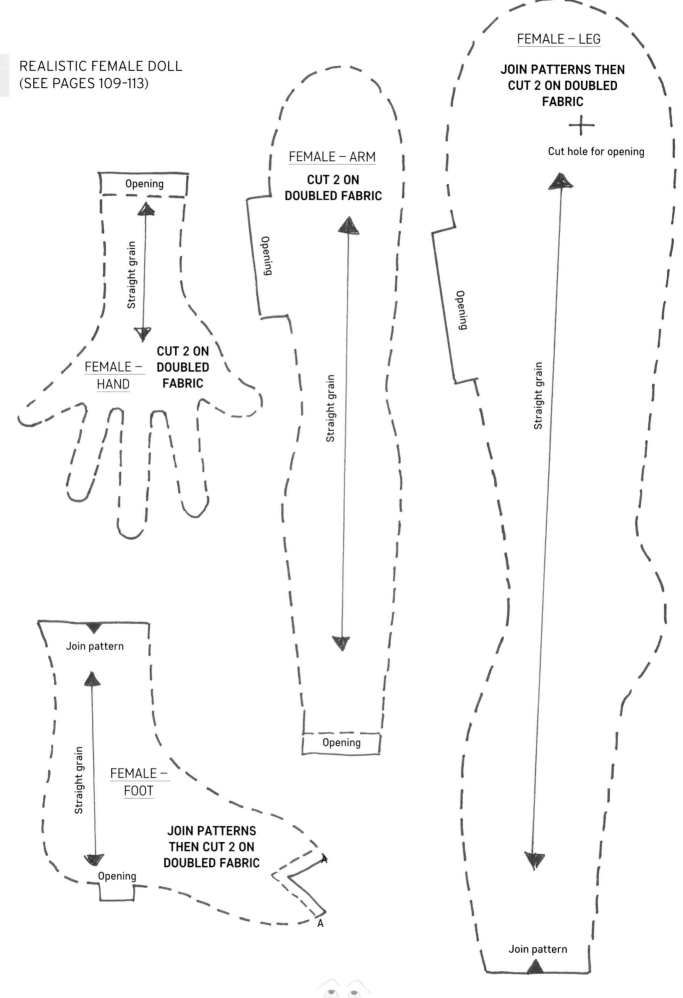

Opening

Straight grain

FEMALE –
HAND

**CUT 2 ON
DOUBLED
FABRIC**

FEMALE – ARM

**CUT 2 ON
DOUBLED FABRIC**

Opening

Straight grain

Opening

FEMALE – LEG

**JOIN PATTERNS THEN
CUT 2 ON DOUBLED
FABRIC**

Cut hole for opening

Opening

Straight grain

Join pattern

Straight grain

FEMALE –
FOOT

**JOIN PATTERNS
THEN CUT 2 ON
DOUBLED FABRIC**

Opening

A

A

Join pattern

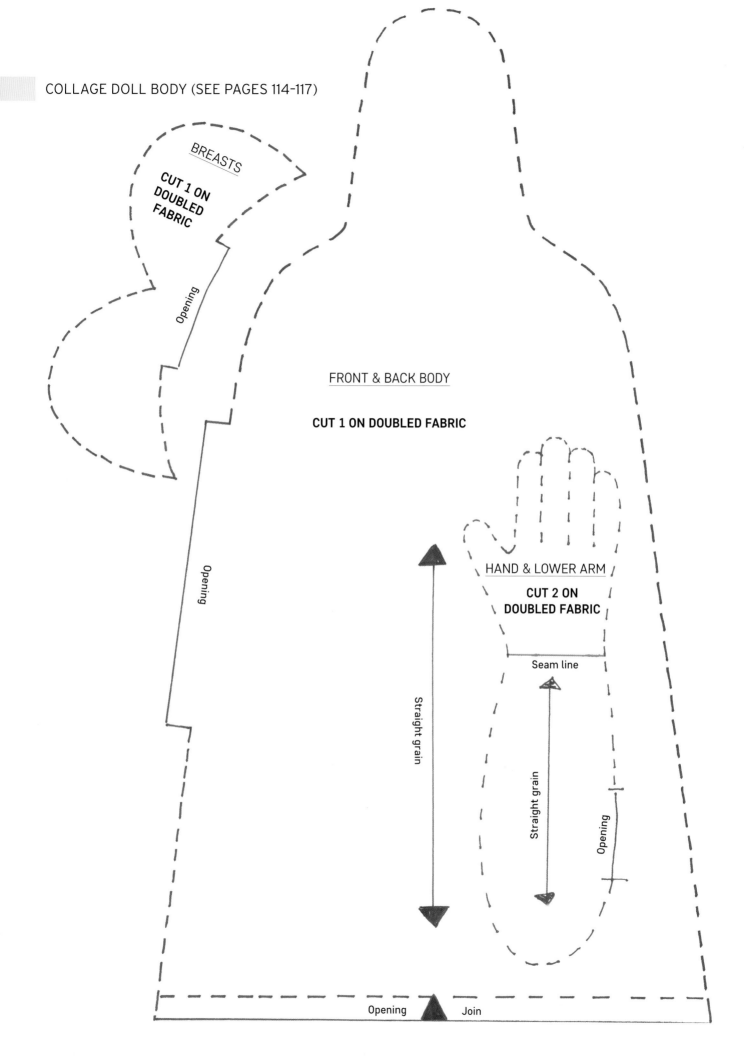

COLLAGE DOLL BODY (SEE PAGES 114–117)

BREASTS

CUT 1 ON DOUBLED FABRIC

Opening

FRONT & BACK BODY

CUT 1 ON DOUBLED FABRIC

Opening

HAND & LOWER ARM

CUT 2 ON DOUBLED FABRIC

Seam line

Straight grain

Straight grain

Opening

Opening   Join

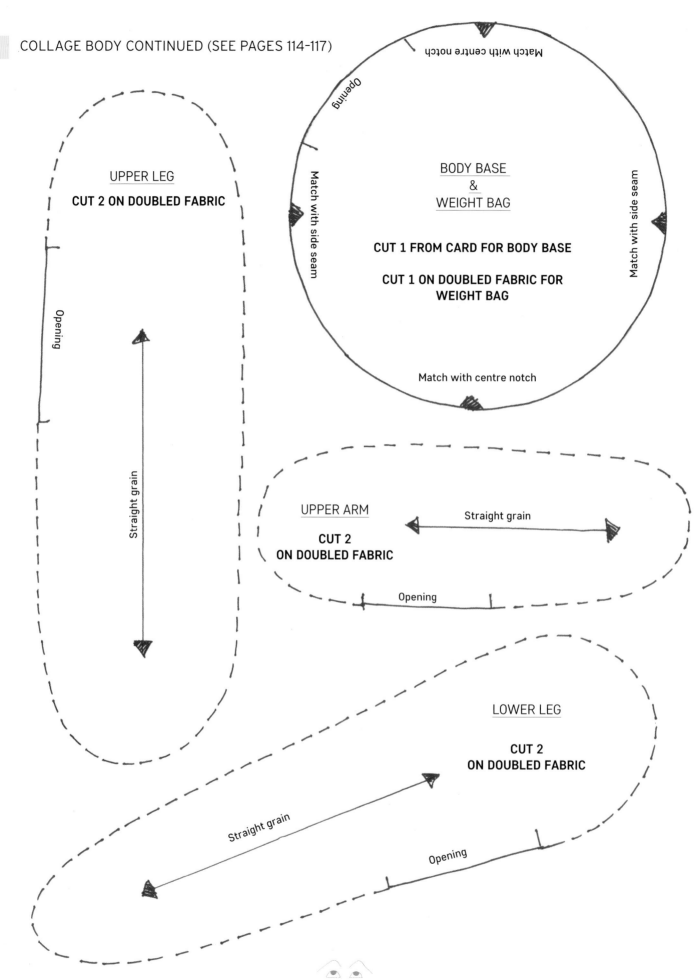

UPPER LEG

CUT 2 ON DOUBLED FABRIC

Opening

Straight grain

BODY BASE
&
WEIGHT BAG

CUT 1 FROM CARD FOR BODY BASE

CUT 1 ON DOUBLED FABRIC FOR WEIGHT BAG

Opening

Match with centre notch

Match with side seam

Match with side seam

Match with centre notch

UPPER ARM

**CUT 2
ON DOUBLED FABRIC**

Straight grain

Opening

LOWER LEG

**CUT 2
ON DOUBLED FABRIC**

Straight grain

Opening